In the Beginning was the Word

In the Beginning was the Word

David Adam
Nicky Gumbel
James Jones
Tim LaHaye & Jerry B. Jenkins
C. S. Lewis
Max Lucado
Frank Morison
Eugene H. Peterson
John R. W. Stott
Philip Yancey

Copyright © 1999 SAM BOOKS

First published in 1999 by SAM BOOKS
Produced courtesy of Paternoster Publishing
PO Box 300, Carlisle, Cumbria, CA3 0QS, UK

Permissions have been granted by the following publishers:
Kingsway Publications Ltd
SPCK
NavPress
Word Publishing
Fount Paperbacks
Zondervan Publishing House
OM Publishing
Inter-Varsity Press
Tyndale House Publishers
The Bible Reading Fellowship
Full copyright details are included at the beginning of each chapter

05 04 03 02 01 00 99   7 6 5 4 3 2 1

British Library Cataloguing in Publication Data
A catalogue record for this book is available from the British Library
ISBN 1-900836-01-7

Typeset by WestKey Ltd, Falmouth, Cornwall
Printed in Great Britain by
Caledonian International Book Manufacturing Ltd, Glasgow

Contents

Foreword

Just as I was about to start writing my own first book, I went along for 'Songs of Praise' to interview Edith Pargeter, the elderly but fascinating writer who was also known as Ellis Peters, the creator of mediaeval sleuth, Brother Cadfael. How could she bring to life the heart and faith of this worldly but deeply spiritual, monk? I shall never forget her answer. 'I am a religious writer,' she said.

'I am a Christian myself, and I hope with all my heart that comes across in everything I write. I can talk about Brother Cadfael's faith, because it is also my own.' Her words became an inspiration to me, a new writer, grappling with how to put across my own faith, and my own experience of meeting so many inspiring people through 'Songs of Praise', so that it would touch others in a relevant and memorable way.

For Edith, and for me, the answer was to write in the form of a novel, knowing that so many of our own questions, answers and commitment are revealed within its pages. Others can inspire in a factual way, sharing how their experience and faith make sense of the dilemmas they see around them.

The World Book Day 'Book of Books' provides a wonderful opportunity to dip into great Christian books and sample the wisdom and insights of some of the most gifted and influential Christian writers of this century. Each chapter reflects a different aspect of what being a Christian is all about. What a marvellous rich variety that leaves you wanting more!

For each of us, faith IS intensely personal – and that's why I believe books written by inspiring, knowledgeable and experienced Christians can make more impression than the most thundering of sermons, and be such a wonderful resource to us all. They're always there when you need them, to challenge, to comfort and console. Some of my best friends are books, and my life is richer for them.

Pam Rhodes

Preface

"Good words are worth much, and cost little."
George Herbert, 17th Century cleric and poet

George Herbert's words are a fitting introduction to this collection of 'good words' by ten of this century's finest Christian authors. Each featured chapter is taken from a 'classic' of its kind, especially selected and compiled to celebrate World Book Day 1999. Here you can sample intriguing words to spark your interest, wise words to stimulate your intellect and encouraging words to build up your faith.

From the master of apologetics, C. S. Lewis, to the biblical interpretation of John Stott, from the clear and incisive thinking of Philip Yancey and Max Lucado, to the depth and understanding of James Jones – each whets our appetite for more.

Frank Morison's investigation into the events of the first Easter has, for decades, helped those seeking the truth. David Adam's ability to draw from the roots of Celtic traditions inspires our prayers while Nicky Gumbel tackles some hard questions. Tim LaHaye and Jerry B. Jenkins' novel points to the future with prophetic overtones.

Finally, a chapter from Eugene H. Peterson shows us that what was true in the first century is still relevant and true for us as we enter the new millennium.

Our thanks go to all authors and publishers for sharing their 'good words' with us.

Questions of Life

Nicky Gumbel

Nicky Gumbel and the *Alpha* Course with which he is associated have helped thousands to a deeper personal understanding of the Christian faith. In *Questions of Life* he tackles the answers to some key questions and in so doing creates a sympathetic, fascinating and immensely readable introduction to Jesus Christ.

ISBN: 0–85476–591–3

Price: £5.99

1

Christianity: Boring, Untrue and Irrelevant?

For many years I had three objections to the Christian faith. First, I thought it was boring. I went to chapel at school and found it very dull. I felt sympathy with Robert Louis Stevenson who once entered in his diary, as if recording an extraordinary phenomenon, 'I have been to Church today, and am not depressed.' In a similar vein, the American humorist, Oliver Wendell Holmes, wrote, 'I might have entered the ministry if certain clergymen I knew had not looked and acted so much like undertakers.' My impression of the Christian faith was that it was dreary and uninspiring.

Secondly, it seemed to me to be untrue. I had intellectual objections to the Christian faith and, rather pretentiously, I called myself a logical determinist. When I was fourteen I wrote an essay in an RE lesson in which I tried to destroy the whole of Christianity and disprove the existence of God. Rather surprisingly, it was put forward for a prize! I had knock-down arguments against the Christian faith and rather enjoyed arguing with Christians, thinking I had won some great victory.

Thirdly, I thought that it was irrelevant. I could not see how something that happened 2,000 years ago and 2,000 miles away in the Middle East could have any relevance to my life in twentieth-century Britain. We often used to sing that much-loved hymn 'Jerusalem' which asks, 'And did those feet in ancient time walk upon England's mountains green?' We all knew that the answer was, 'No, they did not.' It seemed to be totally irrelevant to my life.

I realise, with hindsight, it was partly my fault as I never really listened and was totally ignorant about the Christian faith. There are many people today, in our secularised society, who don't know much about Jesus Christ, or what he did, or anything to do with Christianity. One hospital chaplain listed some of the replies he was given to the question, 'Would you like Holy Communion?' These are some of the answers:

'No thanks, I'm Church of England.'

'No thanks, I asked for Cornflakes.'

'No thanks, I've never been circumcised.'

Christianity is far from boring, it is not untrue and it is not irrelevant. On the contrary, it is exciting, true and relevant. Jesus said, 'I am the way and the truth and the life' (John 14:6). If he was right, and I believe he was, then there can be nothing more important in this life than our response to him.

Direction for a lost world

Men and women were created to live in a relationship with God. Without that relationship there will always be a hunger, an emptiness, a feeling that something is missing. Prince Charles recently spoke of his belief that, for all the advances of science, 'there remains deep in the soul (if I dare use that word), a persistent and unconscious anxiety that something is missing, some ingredient that makes life worth living'.

Bernard Levin, perhaps the greatest columnist of this generation, once wrote an article called 'Life's Great Riddle, and No Time to Find Its Meaning'. In it he spoke of the fact that in spite of his great success as a columnist for over twenty years he feared that he might have 'wasted reality in the chase of a dream'. He wrote:

> To put it bluntly, have I time to discover why I was born before I die? . . . I have not managed to answer the question yet, and however many years I have before me they are certainly not as many as there are behind. There is an obvious danger in leaving it too late . . . why do I *have* to know why I was born? Because, of course, I am unable to believe that it was an accident; and if it wasn't one, it must have a meaning.

He is not a Christian and wrote recently, 'For the fourteen thousandth time, I am not a Christian.' Yet he seems to be only too aware of the inadequate answers to the meaning of life. He wrote some years earlier:

> Countries like ours are full of people who have all the material comforts they desire, together with such non-material blessings as a happy family, and yet lead lives of quiet, and at times noisy, desperation, understanding nothing but the fact that there is a hole inside them and that however much food and drink they pour into it, however many motor cars and television sets they stuff it with, however many well balanced children and loyal friends they parade around the edges of it . . . it aches.

Some people spend much of their lives seeking something that will give meaning and purpose to live. Leo Tolstoy, author of *War and Peace* and *Anna Karenina*, wrote a book called *A Confession* in 1879, in which he tells the story of his search for meaning and purpose in life. He had rejected Christianity as a child. When he left university he sought to get as much pleasure out of life as he could. He entered the social world of Moscow and Petersburg, drinking heavily, living promiscuously, gambling and leading a wild life. But it did not satisfy him.

Then he became ambitious for money. He had inherited an estate and made a large amount of money out of his books. Yet that did not satisfy him either. He sought success, fame and importance. These he also achieved. He wrote what the *Encyclopedia Britannica* describes as 'one of the two or three greatest novels in world literature'. But he was left asking the question, 'Well fine . . . so what?' to which he had no answer.

Then he became ambitious for his family – to give them the best possible life. He married in 1862 and had a kind, loving wife and thirteen children (which, he said, distracted him from any search for the overall meaning of life!). He had achieved all his ambitions and was surrounded by what appeared to be complete happiness. And yet one question brought him to the verge of suicide: 'Is there any meaning in my life which will not be annihilated by the inevitability of death which awaits me?'

He searched for the answer in every field of science and philosophy. The only answer he could find to the question 'Why do I live?' was that 'in the infinity of space and the infinity of time infinitely small particles mutate with infinite complexity'.

As he looked round at his contemporaries he saw that people were not facing up to the first order questions of life ('Where did I come from?', 'Where am I heading?', 'Who am I?', 'What is life about?'). Eventually he found that the peasant people of Russia had been able to answer these questions through their Christian faith and he came to realise that only in Jesus Christ do we find the answer.

Over a hundred years later nothing has changed. Freddie Mercury, the lead singer of the rock group Queen, who died at the end of 1991 wrote in one of his last songs on _The Miracle_ album, 'Does anybody know what we are living for?' In spite of the fact that he had amassed a huge fortune and had attracted thousands of fans, he admitted in an interview shortly before his death that he was desperately lonely. He said, 'You can have everything in the world and still be the loneliest man, and that is the most bitter type of loneliness. Success has brought me world idolisation and millions of pounds, but it's prevented me from having the one thing we all need – a loving, ongoing relationship.'

He was right to speak of an 'ongoing relationship' as the one thing we all need. Yet no human relationship will satisfy entirely. Nor can it be completely ongoing. There always remains something missing. That is because we were created to live in a relationship with God. Jesus said, 'I am the way.' He is the only One who can bring us into that relationship with God that goes on into eternity.

When I was a child our family had an old black and white television set. We could never get a very good picture; it was always fuzzy and used to go into lines. We were quite happy with it since we did not know anything different. One day, we discovered that it needed an outside aerial! Suddenly we found that we could get clear and distinct pictures. Our enjoyment was transformed. Life without a relationship with God through Jesus Christ is like the television without the aerial. Some people seem quite happy, because they don't realise that there is something better. Once we have experienced a relationship with God the purpose and meaning of life should become clear. We see things that we have never seen, and it would be foolish to want to return to the old life. We understand why we were made.

Reality in a confused world

Sometimes people say, 'It does not matter what you believe so long as you are sincere.' But it is possible to be sincerely wrong. Adolf Hitler was sincerely wrong. His beliefs destroyed the lives of millions of people. The Yorkshire Ripper believed that he was doing God's will when he killed prostitutes. He too was sincerely wrong. His beliefs affected his behaviour. These are extreme examples, but they make the point that it matters a great deal what we believe, because what we believe will dictate how we live.

Other people's response to a Christian may be, 'It's great for you, but it is not for me.' This is not a logical position. If Christianity is true, it is of vital importance to every one of us. If it is not true, Christians are deluded and it is not 'great for us' – it is very sad and the sooner we are put right the better. As the writer and scholar C. S. Lewis put it, 'Christianity is a statement which, if false, is of *no* importance, and, if true, of infinite importance. The one thing it cannot be is moderately important.'

Is it true? Is there any evidence? Jesus said, 'I am . . . the truth.' Is there any evidence to support his claim? These are some of the questions which we will be looking at later in the book. The linchpin of Christianity is the resurrection of Jesus Christ and for that there is ample evidence. Professor Thomas Arnold, who as the headmaster of Rugby School revolutionised the concept of English education, was appointed to the chair of modern history at Oxford University. He was certainly a man well acquainted with the value of evidence in determining historical facts, and he said:

> I have been used for many years to studying the histories of other times, and to examining and weighing the evidence of those who have written about them, and I know of no one fact in the history of mankind which is proved by better and fuller evidence of every sort, to the understanding of a fair inquirer, than the great sign which God has given us that Christ died and rose again from the dead.

As we shall see later in the book, there is a great deal of evidence that Christianity is true. Yet, when Jesus said, 'I am . . . the truth,' he meant more than intellectual truth. The original word for truth carries with it the notion of doing or experiencing the truth. There is something more than an intellectual acceptance of the truth of Christianity, and that is the knowledge of Jesus Christ who is *the* truth.

Suppose that before I met my wife Pippa I had read a book about her. Then, after I had finished reading the book I thought, 'This sounds like a wonderful woman. This is the person I want to marry.' There would be a big difference in my state of mind then – intellectually convinced that she was a wonderful person – and my state of mind now after the experience of many years of marriage from which I can say, 'I know she is a wonderful person.' When a Christian says, in relation to his faith, 'I know

Jesus is the truth,' he does not mean only that he knows intellectually that he is the truth, but that he has experienced Jesus as the truth. As we come into relationship with the One who is the truth, our perceptions change, and we begin to understand the truth about the world around us.

Life in a dark world

Jesus said, 'I am . . . the life.' In Jesus we find life where previously there has been guilt, addiction, fear and the prospect of death. It is true that all of us were created in the image of God and there is, therefore, something noble about all human beings. However, we are all also fallen – we are born with a propensity to do evil. In every human being the image of God has been to a greater or lesser extent tarnished, and in some cases almost eradicated, by sin. Good and bad, strength and weakness coexist in all human beings. Alexander Solzhenitsyn, the Russian writer, said, 'The line separating good and evil passes, not through states, nor through classes, nor between political parties . . . but right through every human heart and through all human hearts.'

I used to think I was a 'nice' person – because I didn't rob banks or commit other serious crimes. Only when I began to see my life alongside the life of Jesus Christ did I realise how much there was wrong. Many others have had this same experience. C. S. Lewis wrote: 'For the first time I examined myself with a seriously practical purpose. And there I found what appalled me; a zoo of lusts, a bedlam of ambitions, a nursery of fears, a harem of fondled hatreds. My name was Legion.'

We all need forgiveness and only in Christ can it be found. Marghanita Laski, the humanist, debating on television with a Christian, made an amazing confession. She said, 'What I envy most about you Christians is your forgiveness.' Then she added, rather pathetically, 'I have no one to forgive me.'

What Jesus did when he was crucified for us was to pay the penalty for all the things that we have done wrong. We will look at this subject in Chapter 4 in more detail. We will see that he died to remove our guilt, to set us free from addiction, fear and ultimately death. He died instead of us.

On 31st July 1991 a remarkable event was celebrated. On the last day of July 1941 the Auschwitz sirens announced the escape of a prisoner. As a reprisal, ten of his fellow prisoners would die – a long, slow starvation, buried alive in a specially constructed, concrete bunker.

So all day, tortured by sun, hunger and fear, the men waited as the German commandant and his Gestapo assistant walked between the ranks to select, quite arbitrarily, the chosen ten. As the commandant pointed to one man, Francis Gajowniczek, he cried out in despair, 'My poor wife and children.' At that moment the unimpressive figure of a man with sunken eyes and round glasses in wire frames stepped out of line and took off his cap. 'What does this Polish pig want?' asked the commandant.

'I am a Catholic priest; I want to die for that man. I am old, he has a wife and children . . . I have no one,' said Father Maximilian Kolbe.

'Accepted,' retorted the commandant, and moved on.

That night, nine men and one priest went to the starvation bunker. Normally they would tear each other apart like cannibals. Not so this time. While they had strength, lying naked on the floor, the men prayed and sang hymns. After two weeks, three of the men and Father Maximilian were still alive. The bunker was required for others, so on 14th August, the remaining four were disposed of. At 12.50 pm, after two weeks in the starvation bunker and still conscious, the Polish priest was finally given an injection of phenol and died at the age of forty-seven.

On 10th October 1982 in St Peter's Square, Rome, Father Maximilian's death was put in its proper perspective. Present in the crowd of 150,000 was Francis Gajowniczek, his wife, his children, and his children's children – for indeed, many had been saved by that one man. The Pope describing Father Maximilian's death said, 'This was victory won over all the systems of contempt and hate in man – a victory like that won by our Lord Jesus Christ.'

Jesus' death was, indeed, even more amazing because Jesus died, not just for one man, but for every single individual in the world. If you or I had been the only person in the world, Jesus Christ would have died instead of us to remove our guilt. When our guilt is removed we have a new life.

Jesus not only died for us, he also rose again from the dead for us. In this act he defeated death. Most rational people are aware of the inevitability of death, although today some people make bizarre attempts to avoid it. *The Church of England Newspaper* described one such attempt:

In 1960 Californian millionaire James McGill died. He left detailed instructions that his body should be preserved and frozen in the hope that one day scientists might discover a cure for the disease that killed him. There are hundreds of people in Southern California who have put hopes of one day living again in this process which freezes and preserves human bodies. The latest development in Cryonics technology is called neuro-suspension which preserves just the human head. One reason why it is becoming popular is that it is much cheaper than preserving and maintaining a whole body. It reminds me of Woody Allen in *Sleeper*, where he preserved his nose.

Such attempts to avoid the inevitability of death are plainly absurd and, indeed, unnecessary. Jesus came to bring us 'eternal life'. Eternal life is a quality of life which comes from living in a relationship with God and Jesus Christ (John 17:3). Jesus never promised anyone an easy life, but he promised fullness of life (John 10:10). This new quality of life starts now and goes on into eternity. Our time on earth is relatively short, but eternity is vast. Through Jesus, who said, 'I am . . . the life' we can not only enjoy fullness of life here, but we can be sure that it will never end.

Christianity is not boring; it is about living life to the full. It is not untrue; it is *the* truth. It is not irrelevant; it transforms the whole of our lives. The theologian and philosopher Paul Tillich described the human condition as one that always involves three fears: fear about meaninglessness, fear about death and fear about guilt. Jesus Christ meets each of these fears head on. He is vital to every one of us because he is 'the way, and the truth, and the life'.

The Rhythm of Life

David Adam

'To survive the dry times as well as the times of richness, we need to have an overriding rhythm of prayer.' So says David Adam, Vicar of Holy Island who uses his gift for composing prayers in the Celtic tradition to bring us this inspiring collection of prayers and readings.

ISBN: 0–281–04893–2

Price: £4.99

First published in 1996 by SPCK,
Holy Trinty Church, Marylebone Road, London NW1 4DU
All rights reserved

Introduction

The rhythm of life on the island of Lindisfarne where I live is ordered not only by the tides and the seasons but by the daily ringing of the church bell for prayer. People are made aware of the fact that prayer is being said early in the morning and again in the evening. Many of the visitors to the island come and share in the daily prayers. Every day we say Morning and Evening Prayer and celebrate the Eucharist, and several people have expressed a wish that they could continue this pattern in some way when they return to their homes. They would like to establish fixed times for prayer which will enrich the whole day and guide them through it, while also keeping a link with the whole wide church at prayer. Some have asked for a pattern of prayer for the week. Out of this has arisen this series of 'little offices' to help people to rejoice constantly in the presence of the living God.

The use of the word 'office' dates back to the beginnings of the monastic movement in the early centuries of the church, and was originally used to acknowledge the *officium*, or duty, of each Christian to pray daily with the whole church. The daily office was meant to meet the need for more public prayers and psalms than were found in the

Communion service, prayers which could be said by people at home, as well as by the monks in church. Because most people could not read, and in any case books were not available, the office by its nature needed to be short, and something that could easily be committed to memory. It was intended to be part of the public daily prayers of the church, and to build up shared worship in the community.

The acts of worship in this book are designed to be complete in themselves, and simple to use. The Bible readings are purposely short so that they can be memorized. Likewise, the prayers are written in such a way that they can soon be learned off by heart, simply by regular recitation. I am a great believer in 'recital theology' – that is, to get the word off the page and into the mind and the heart. For this reason it is good whenever possible to say the prayers aloud. By reciting aloud, we use our eyes, mouth and ears as well as our minds. Reading aloud produces a physical vibration that affects not only our ears but our heart and our mind also, so that when we hear the words in a different context an echoing chord is struck in our being, setting off a whole melody of associations. Once we have words in our heart, a phrase, or even a single word, can pluck at our heartstrings and cause us to react.

When we celebrate in worship the mighty acts of God, we are not so much concerned with remembering as with entering into the events; we are emphasising the eternal rather than the historical. We need to be open to the fact that what we are celebrating, because it is eternal, is here and now. It is *now* that our Lord comes, it is *now* that he is born among us, it is *now* that he is seen among us, it is *now* that the risen Lord appears. In the same way it is *now* that the Father is creating and re-creating. It is *now* that the Spirit descends. Our celebrations tune us in to the eternal events, allow us to respond to them and to carry that response into our daily living. Thus the rhythm of prayer resonates throughout the day.

We are not just reading or acting out the great events of God, we are partaking in them. We celebrate Advent with the assurance that our Lord comes, and comes to us here and now. In the same manner we seek to meet the incarnate Lord who dwells among us. The betrayal, rejection, crucifixion and death of our Lord weave their way through our streets, our homes and our lives. We need to be sensitive to the redeeming love and salvation that is now at work in us, as we also need to be aware of the many deaths and resurrections that are experienced by us. I believe in the resurrection of the body for it is an on-going fact. The whole of the liturgical year is a mystery, joyful, sorrowful and glorious, that is at work in us and through us. We need to become more aware of these rhythms in our life.

Each 'little office' should have some link with Sunday worship, so that the one enriches the other. One of the great weaknesses of the church today is that people have stopped praying in their homes; or if they do pray, their prayer often has no link with the church or liturgy and so does not resonate with them. Without daily Bible reading and ordered prayer, it is hard for our Sunday worship to strike a chord. But if through daily prayer and a build-up of images the Sunday worship plucks at certain strings, then all are enriched. Once we have built up a collection of phrases and sayings which we have meditated on, every time they are used they echo and re-echo in the depths of our lives. When we have the office by heart we can use it at any spare minute in the day until it truly vibrates in our life – better, until He truly vibrates in our life.

Sunday Morning – Resurrection

Jesus Christ is risen from the dead. Alleluia!

(*Silence*)

Rejoice, heavenly powers! Sing, choirs of angels! Alleluia!
Christ our King is risen. Alleluia!
Exult, all creation! Rejoice, O earth, in shining splendour!
   Alleluia!
Christ our King is risen. Alleluia!
Christ has conquered! Glory fills you!
Christ our King is risen. Alleluia!
Darkness vanishes forever! Christ dispels the darkness of
   our night! Alleluia!
Christ our King is risen. Alleluia!

PSALM 100

Christ is risen. Alleluia!

Be joyful in the Lord, all you lands;
serve the Lord with gladness
and come before his presence with a song.

Know this: The Lord himself is God;
he himself has made us and we are his;
we are his people and the sheep of his pasture.

Enter his gates with thanksgiving;
go into his courts with praise;
give thanks to him and call upon his name.

For the Lord is good; his mercy is everlasting;
and his faithfulness endures from age to age.

Christ is risen. Alleluia!

JOHN 11.25–6

Jesus said . . . 'I am the resurrection and the life. Those who believe in me, even though they die, will live, and everyone who lives and believes in me will never die.'

THE SONG OF CHRIST'S GLORY

At the name of Jesus every knee should bow.

Christ Jesus was in the form of God:
but he did not cling to equality with God.
At the name of Jesus every knee should bow.

He emptied himself, taking the form of a servant:
and was born in the likeness of men.
At the name of Jesus every knee should bow.

Being found in human form he humbled himself:
and became obedient unto death, even death on a cross.
At the name of Jesus every knee should bow.

Therefore God has highly exalted him:
and bestowed on him a name above every name;
At the name of Jesus every knee should bow.

that at the name of Jesus every knee should bow:
in heaven and on earth and under the earth;
At the name of Jesus every knee should bow.

and every tongue confess that Jesus Christ is Lord:
to the glory of God the Father.
At the name of Jesus every knee should bow.

Glory be to the Father, and to the Son;
and to the Holy Spirit:
as it was in the beginning, is now;
and shall be for ever. Amen.

At the name of Jesus every knee should bow.

Lord, have mercy upon us.
Christ, have mercy upon us.
Lord, have mercy upon us.

Our Father . . .

That we may rejoice in the resurrection,
Risen Christ, give us hope.
That we may know that you have conquered death,
Risen Christ, give us hope.
That we may know that you have triumphed over the
grave,
Risen Christ, give us hope.
That those in doubt and despair may see your light,
Risen Christ, give us hope.
That those who are troubled in mind may know your
peace,
Risen Christ, give us hope.
That those in pain and distress may know your presence,
Risen Christ, give us hope.
That those caring for the terminally ill may know your
power,
Risen Christ, give us hope.
That those who mourn may discover the joy of life eternal,
Risen Christ, give us hope.

Almighty Father, who in your great mercy made glad the
disciples with the sight of the risen Lord: give us such
knowledge of his presence with us, that we may be
strengthened and sustained by his risen life and serve you
continually in righteousness and truth: through Jesus Christ
our Lord.
Amen.*

The God of hope, who brought again from the dead that great Shepherd of the sheep, Jesus Christ, fill us with all joy and peace in believing.

Sunday Midday – Resurrection

Alleluia! Christ is risen.
He is risen indeed. Alleluia!

(*Silence*)

He has conquered death. **Alleluia!**
He has triumphed over the grave.
    Alleluia!
He has defeated hell. **Alleluia!**
He has risen again. **Alleluia!**
Christ is alive. **Alleluia!**

PSALM 23

The Lord is my shepherd; I will fear no evil.

The Lord is my shepherd;
I shall not be in want.

He makes me lie down in green pastures;
and leads me beside still waters.

He revives my soul
and guides me along right pathways for his name's sake.

Though I walk through the valley of the shadow of death, I
    shall fear no evil;
for you are with me; your rod and your staff, they comfort
    me.

You spread a table before me in the presence of those who
    trouble me;
You have anointed my head with oil, and my cup is
    running over.

Surely goodness and mercy shall follow me all the days of
    my life,
and I will dwell in the house of the Lord for ever.

The Lord is my shepherd; I will fear no evil.

ROMANS 6.3–6
Do you not know that all of us who have been baptized
into Christ Jesus were baptized into his death? Therefore
we have been buried with him by baptism into death, so
that, just as Christ was raised from the dead by the glory of
the Father, so we too might walk in newness of life.

GLORY AND HONOUR

Glory to God in the highest.

Glory and honour and power:
are yours by right, O Lord our God:

for you created all things:
and by your will they have their being.

Glory and honour and power:
are yours by right, O Lamb who was slain;

for by your blood you ransomed men for God:
from every race and language, from every people and
    nation,

to make them a kingdom of priests:
to stand and serve before our God.

To him who sits on the throne, and to the Lamb:
be praise and honour, glory and might, for ever and ever.
   Amen.

Glory to God in the highest.

Risen Lord, we pray that you will uphold all who are
   down.
Lord, have mercy.
Upon the world's poor and the unemployed,
Lord, have mercy.
Upon the homeless and the refugee,
Lord, have mercy.
Upon the war torn and the oppressed,
Christ, have mercy.
Upon the depressed and the despairing,
Christ, have mercy.
Upon the sinful and the sorrowful,
Christ, have mercy.
Upon the sick and the suffering,
Lord, have mercy.
Upon the diseased and the disgraced,
Lord, have mercy.
Upon the lonely and the dying,
Lord, have mercy.

Our Father . . .

Lord of all life and power, who through the mighty resurrection of your Son overcame the old order of sin and death
to make all things new in him: grant that we, being dead to
sin and alive to you in Jesus Christ, may reign with him in
glory; to whom with you and the Holy Spirit be praise and
honour, glory and might, now and in all eternity. **Amen.**★

May you find in Christ Jesus, risen from the dead, a sure ground for your faith, a firm support for your hope, the assurance of sins forgiven, and life that is eternal.

Sunday Evening – Resurrection

Worthy is the Lamb who was slain to receive power and riches, wisdom and strength, and honour and glory and blessing. Alleluia!

(*Silence*)

That we may know you as the risen Lord,
Hear us, risen Christ.
That in you the downtrodden may find hope,
Hear us, risen Christ.
That in you the darkened lives may find light,
Hear us, risen Christ.
That in you we may rejoice that life is eternal,
Hear us, risen Christ.

PSALM 103.1–8, 19–22

Bless the Lord, O my soul.

Bless the Lord, O my soul,
and all that is within me, bless his holy name.

Bless the Lord, O my soul,
and forget not all his benefits.

He forgives all your sins
and heals all your infirmities;

He redeems your life from the grave
and crowns you with mercy and loving-kindness;

He satisfies you with good things,
and your youth is renewed like an eagle's.

The Lord executes righteousness
and judgement for all who are oppressed.

He made his way known to Moses
and his works to the children of Israel.

The Lord is full of compassion and mercy,
slow to anger and of great kindness . . .

The Lord has set his throne in heaven,
and his kingship has dominion over all.

Bless the Lord, you angels of his,
you mighty ones who do his bidding,
and hearken to the voice of his word.

Bless the Lord, all you his hosts,
you ministers of his who do his will.

Bless the Lord, all you works of his,
in all places of his dominion;
bless the Lord, O my soul.

Bless the Lord, O my soul.

JOHN 20.19
When it was evening on that day, the first day of the week,
and the doors of the house where the disciples had met were
locked for fear of the Jews, Jesus came and stood among
them and said, 'Peace be with you.' After he said this, he
showed them his hands and his side. Then the disciples
rejoiced when they saw the Lord.

BLESSED BE GOD
1 PETER 1.3–5

Blessed be God. Alleluia!

Blessed be the God and Father of our Lord Jesus Christ!
Blessed be God. Alleluia!

By his great mercy he has given us a new birth into a living
　　hope, through the resurrection of Jesus Christ from the
　　dead;
Blessed be God. Alleluia!

and into an inheritance that is imperishable, undefiled, and
　　unfading, kept in heaven for you;
Blessed be God. Alleluia!

who are being protected by the power of God through
　　faith, for a salvation ready to be revealed in the last
　　time.
Blessed be God. Alleluia!

Lord, have mercy . . .

Our Father . . .

Abide with us, Lord, for it is toward the evening and the
day is far spent: abide with us, and with your whole church.
Abide with us in the evening of the day, in the evening of
life, in the evening of the world. Abide with us in your
grace and mercy, in your holy Word and Sacrament, in
your comfort and your blessing. Abide with us in the night
of distress and fear, in the night of doubt and temptation, in
the night of bitter death, when these shall overtake us.
Abide with us and all your faithful ones, O Lord, in time
and in eternity.

The peace and the power of the presence of the risen Lord
be upon you and remain with you always.

Sunday Night – Resurrection

Almighty God, from whose love neither life nor death can
separate us: let the whole company of heaven praise you; let
the whole church throughout the world praise you. Let us
this night praise you.

(*Silence*)

By your death upon the cross
Raise us, good Lord.
By your burial in the grave
Raise us, good Lord.
By your descending into hell
Raise us, good Lord.
By your mighty resurrection
Raise us, good Lord.
By your conquering death
Raise us, good Lord.
By your risen appearances
Raise us, good Lord.
By your presence among us
Raise us, good Lord.

PSALM 113

Praise the name of the Lord. Alleluia!

Alleluia!
Give praise, you servants of the Lord;
praise the name of the Lord.

Let the name of the Lord be blessed;
from this time forth for evermore.

From the rising of the sun to its going down
let the name of the Lord be praised.

The Lord is high above all nations,
and his glory above the heavens.

Who is like the Lord our God, who sits enthroned on high,
but stoops to behold the heavens and the earth?

He takes up the weak out of the dust
and lifts up the poor from the ashes.

He sets them with the princes,
with the princes of his people.

He makes the woman of a childless house
to be a joyful mother of children.

Praise the name of the Lord. Alleluia!

1 PETER 1.3–5
Blessed be the God and Father of our Lord Jesus Christ! By
his great mercy he has given us a new birth into a living
hope through the resurrection of Jesus Christ from the
dead, and into an inheritance that is imperishable, undefiled, and unfading, kept in heaven for you, who are being
protected by the power of God through faith for a salvation
ready to be revealed in the last time.

GREAT AND WONDERFUL

Great and wonderful is our God. Alleluia!

Great and wonderful are your deeds, Lord God the
   Almighty:
just and true are your ways, O king of the nations.

Who shall not revere and praise your name,
O Lord?
for you alone are holy.

All nations shall come and worship in your presence:
for your just dealings have been revealed.

To him who sits upon the throne, and to the Lamb:

be praise and honour, glory and might, for ever and ever.
   Amen.

Great and wonderful is our God. Alleluia!

Lord, have mercy . . .

Our Father . . .

With all who are in darkness and weariness
Stand among us in your risen power.
With all who are in doubt and despair
Stand among us in your risen power.
With all who are in trouble and fearfulness
Stand among us in your risen power.
With all who are in sickness and weakness
Stand among us in your risen power.
With all who are frail and at the point of death
Stand among us in your risen power.

Risen Lord, light of all peoples, who on the third day rose
again from the dead, come, stand among us: dispel the

darkness of night with your celestial brightness, that we may walk before you as in the day, and as children of light; to the glory of your name, risen Lord, with the Father and the Holy Spirit one God for ever and ever. **Amen**.

Christ, risen in glory, scatter the darkness before us, that we may walk as children of light until we come to that light which is eternal.

The Message

Eugene H. Peterson

Written in the rhythm and style of contemporary language, *The Message* blends accurate scholarship and vivid expressions to help you experience first-hand the same power and directness that motivated the original readers of the New Testament. You'll be surprised and startled by this fresh approach to God's Word.

ISBN: 1-57683-102-7

Price: £5.99

Introduction
John

In Genesis, the first book of the Bible, God is presented as speaking the creation into existence. God speaks the word and it happens: heaven and earth, ocean and stream, trees and grass, birds and fish, animals and humans. Everything, seen and unseen, called into being by God's spoken word.

In deliberate parallel to the opening words of Genesis, John presents God as speaking salvation into existence. This time God's word takes on human form and enters history in the person of Jesus speaks the word and it happens: forgiveness and judgment, healing and illumination, mercy and grace, joy and love, freedom and resurrection. Everything broken and fallen, sinful and diseased, called into salvation by God's spoken word.

For, somewhere along the line things went wrong (Genesis tells that story, too) and are in desperate need of fixing. The fixing is all accomplished by speaking – God speaking salvation into being in the person of Jesus. Jesus, in this account, not only speaks the word of God; he is the Word of God.

Keeping company with these words, we begin to realize that our words are more important than we ever

supposed. Saying 'I believe,' for instance, marks the difference between life and death. Our words accrue dignity
and gravity in conversations with Jesus. For Jesus doesn't
impose salvation as a solution; he *narrates* salvation into
being through leisurely conversation, intimate personal
relationships, compassionate responses, passionate prayer,
and – putting it all together – a sacrificial death. We don't
casually walk away from words like that.

The Life-Light

1 The Word was first,
    the Word present to God,
    God present to the Word.
The Word was God,
    in readiness for God from day one.

Everything was created through him;
    nothing – not one thing! –
    came into being without him.
What came into existence was Life,
    and the Life was Light to live by.
The Life-Light blazed out of the darkness;
    the darkness couldn't put it out.

There once was a man, his name John, sent by God to
point out the way to the Life-Light. He came to show everyone where to look, who to believe in. John was not himself
the Light; he was there to show the way to the Light.

The Life-Light was the real thing:
    Every person entering Life

he brings into Light.
He was in the world,
    the world was there through him,
    and yet the world didn't even notice.
He came to his own people,
    but they didn't want him.
But whoever did want him,
    who believed he was who he claimed
    and would do what he said,
He made to be their true selves,
    their child-of-God selves.
These are the God-begotten,
    not blood-begotten,
    not flesh-begotten,
    not sex-begotten.

The Word became flesh and blood,
    and moved into the neighborhood.
We saw the glory with our own eyes,
    the one-of-a-kind glory,
    like Father, like Son,
Generous inside and out,
    true from start to finish

John pointed him out and called, 'This is the One! The One I told you was coming after me but in fact was ahead of me. He has always been ahead of me, has always had the first word.'

We all live off his generous bounty,
    gift after gift after gift.
We got the basics from Moses,
    and then this exuberant giving and receiving,

This endless knowing and understanding –
    all this came through Jesus, the Messiah.
No one has ever seen God,
    not so much as a glimpse.
This one-of-a-kind God-Expression,
    who exists at the very heart of the Father,
    has made him plain as day.

Thunder in the Desert

When Jews from Jerusalem sent a group of priests and officials to ask John who he was, he was completely honest. He didn't evade the question. He told the plain truth: 'I am not the Messiah.'

They pressed him, 'Who, then? Elijah?'

'I am not.'

'The Prophet?'

'No.'

Exasperated, they said, 'Who, then? We need an answer for those who sent us. Tell us something – anything! – about yourself.'

'I'm thunder in the desert: "Make the road straight for God!" I'm doing what the prophet Isaiah preached.'

Those sent to question him were from the Pharisee party. Now they had a question of their own: 'If you're neither the Messiah, nor Elijah, nor the Prophet, why do you baptize?'

John answered, 'I only baptize using water. A person you don't recognize has taken his stand in your midst. He comes after me, but he is not in second place to me. I'm not even worthy to hold his coat for him.'

These conversations took place in Bethany on the other side of the Jordan, where John was baptizing at the time.

The God-Revealer

The very next day John saw Jesus coming toward him and yelled out, 'Here he is, God's Passover Lamb! He forgives the sins of the world! This is the man I've been talking about, "the One who comes after me but is really ahead of me." I knew nothing about who he was – only this: that my task has been to get Israel ready to recognize him as the God-Revealer. That is why I came here baptizing with water, giving you a good bath and scrubbing sins from your life so you can get a fresh start with God.'

John clinched his witness with this: 'I watched the Spirit, like a dove flying down out of the sky, making himself at home in him. I repeat, I know nothing about him except this: The One who authorized me to baptize with water told me, "The One on whom you see the Spirit come down and stay, this One will baptize with the Holy Spirit." That's exactly what I saw happen, and I'm telling you, there's no question about it: *This* is the Son of God.'

Come, See for Yourself

The next day John was back at his post with two disciples, who were watching. He looked up, saw Jesus walking nearby, and said, 'Here he is, God's Passover Lamb.'

The two disciples heard him and went after Jesus. Jesus looked over his shoulder and said to them, 'What are you after?'

They said, 'Rabbi' (which means 'Teacher'), 'where are you staying?'

He replied, 'Come along and see for yourself.'

They came, saw where he was living, and ended up staying with him for the day. It was late afternoon when this happened.

Andrew, Simon Peter's brother, was one of the two who heard John's witness and followed Jesus. The first thing he did after finding where Jesus lived was find his own brother, Simon, telling him, 'We've found the Messiah' (that is, 'Christ'). He immediately led him to Jesus.

Jesus took one look up and said, 'You're John's son, Simon? From now on your name is Cephas' (or Peter, which means 'Rock').

The next day Jesus decided to go to Galilee. When he got there, he ran across Philip and said, 'Come, follow me.' (Philip's home-town was Bethsaida, the same as Andrew and Peter.)

Philip went and found Nathanael and told him, 'We've found the One Moses wrote of in the Law, the One preached by the prophets. It's *Jesus*, Joseph's son, the one from Nazareth!' Nathanael said, 'Nazareth? You've got to be kidding.'

But Philip said, 'Come, see for yourself.'

When Jesus saw him coming he said, 'There's a real Israelite, not a false bone in his body.'

Nathanael said, 'Where did you get that idea? You don't know me.'

Jesus answered, 'One day, long before Philip called you here, I saw you under the fig tree.'

Nathanael exclaimed, 'Rabbi! You are the Son of God, the King of Israel!'

Jesus said, 'You've become a believer simply because I say I saw you one day sitting under the fig tree? You haven't seen anything yet! Before this is over you're going to see heaven open and God's angels descending to the Son of Man and ascending again.'

From Water to Wine

2 Three days later there was a wedding in the village of Cana in Galilee. Jesus' mother was there. Jesus and his disciples were guests also. When they started running low on wine at the wedding banquet, Jesus' mother told him, 'They're just about out of wine.'

Jesus said, 'Is that any of our business, Mother – yours or mine? This isn't my time. Don't push me.'

She went ahead anyway, telling the servants, 'Whatever he tells you, do it.'

Six stoneware water pots were there, used by the Jews for ritual washings. Each held twenty to thirty gallons. Jesus ordered the servants, 'Fill the pots with water.' And they filled them to the brim.

'Now fill your pitchers and take them to the host,' Jesus said, and they did.

When the host tasted the water that had become wine (he didn't know what had just happened but the servants, of course, knew), he called out to the bridegroom, 'Everybody I know begins with their finest wines and after the guests have had their fill brings in the cheap stuff. But you've saved the best till now!'

This act in Cana of Galilee was the first sign Jesus gave, the first glimpse of his glory. And his disciples believed in him.

After this he went down to Capernaum along with his mother, brothers, and disciples, and stayed several days.

Tear Down this Temple . . .

When the Passover Feast, celebrated each spring by the Jews, was about to take place, Jesus traveled up to Jerusalem. He found the Temple teeming with people selling cattle and sheep and doves. The loan sharks were also there in full strength.

Jesus put together a whip out of strips of leather and chased them out of the Temple, stampeding the sheep and cattle, upending the tables of the loan sharks, spilling coins left and right. He told the dove merchants, 'Get your things out of here! Stop turning my Father's house into a shopping mall!' That's when his disciples remembered the Scripture, 'Zeal for your house consumes me.'

But the Jews were upset. They asked, 'What credentials can you present to justify this?' Jesus answered, 'Tear down this Temple and in three days I'll put it back together.'

They were indignant: 'It took forty-six years to build this Temple, and you're going to rebuild it in three days?' But Jesus was talking about his body as the Temple. Later, after he was raised from the dead, his disciples remembered he had said this. They then put two and two together and believed both what was written in Scripture and what Jesus had said.

During the time he was in Jerusalem, those days of the Passover Feast, many people noticed the signs he was displaying and, seeing they pointed straight to God, entrusted their lives to him. But Jesus didn't entrust his life to them. He knew them inside and out, knew how untrustworthy they were. He didn't need any help in seeing right through them.

Born From Above

3 There was a man of the Pharisee sect, Nicodemus, a prominent leader among the Jews. Late one night he visited Jesus and said, 'Rabbi, we all know you're a teacher straight from God. No one could do all the God-pointing, God-revealing acts you do if God weren't in on it.'

Jesus said, 'You're absolutely right. Take it from me: Unless a person is born from above, it's not possible to see what I'm pointing to – to God's kingdom.'

'How can anyone,' said Nicodemus, 'be born who has already been born and grown up? You can't re-enter your mother's womb and be born again. What are you saying with this "born-from-above" talk?'

Jesus said, 'You're not listening. Let me say it again. Unless a person submits to this original creation – the "wind hovering over the water" creation, the invisible moving the visible, a baptism into a new life – it's not possible to enter God's kingdom. When you look at a baby, it's just that: a body you can look at and touch. But the person who takes shape within is formed by something you can't see and touch – the Spirit – and becomes a living spirit.

'So don't be so surprised when I tell you that you have to be "born from above" – out of this world, so to speak. You know well enough how the wind blows this way and that. You hear it rustling through the trees, but you have no idea where it comes from or where it's headed next. That's the way it is with everyone "born from above" by the wind of God, the Spirit of God.'

Nicodemus asked, 'What do you mean by this? How does this happen?'

Jesus said, 'You're a respected teacher of Israel and you don't know these basics? Listen carefully. I'm speaking sober truth to you. I speak only of what I know by experience; I give witness only to what I have seen with my own eyes. There is nothing second-hand here, no hearsay. Yet instead of facing the evidence and accepting it, you procrastinate with questions. If I tell you things that are plain as the hand before your face and you don't believe me, what use is there in telling you of things you can't see, the things of God?

'No one has ever gone up into the presence of God except the One who came down from that Presence, the Son of Man. In the same way that Moses lifted the serpent in the desert so people could have something to see and then believe, it is necessary for the Son of Man to be lifted up – and everyone who looks up to him, trusting and expectant, will gain a real life, eternal life.

'This is how much God loved the world: He gave his Son, his one and only Son. And this is why: so that no one need be destroyed; by believing in him, anyone can have a whole and lasting life. God didn't go to all the trouble of sending his Son merely to point an accusing finger, telling the world how bad it was. He came to help, to put the world right again. Anyone who trusts in him is acquitted; anyone who refuses to trust him has long since been under the death sentence without knowing it. And why? Because of that person's failure to believe in the one-of-a-kind Son of God when introduced to him.

'This is the crisis we're in: God-light streamed into the world, but men and women everywhere ran for the darkness. They went for the darkness because they were not really interested in pleasing God. Everyone who makes a practice of doing evil, addicted to denial and illusion, hates God-light and won't come near it, fearing a painful exposure. But anyone working and living in truth and reality welcomes God-light so the work can be seen for the God-work it is.'

The Bridegroom's Friend

After this conversation, Jesus went on with his disciples into the Judean countryside and relaxed with them there. He was also baptizing. At the same time, John was baptizing over at Aenon near Salim, where water was abundant. This was before John was thrown into jail. John's disciples got into an argument with the establishment Jews over the nature of baptism. They came to John and said, 'Rabbi, you know the one who was with you on the other side of the Jordan? The one you authorized with your witness? Well, he's now competing with us. He's baptizing, too, and everyone's going to him instead of us.'

John answered, 'It's not possible for a person to succeed – I'm talking about *eternal* success – without heaven's help. You yourselves were there when I made it public that I was not the Messiah but simply the one sent ahead of him to get things ready. The one who gets the bride is, by definition, the bridegroom. And the bridegroom's friend, his 'best man' – that's me – in place at his side where he can hear every word, is genuinely happy. How could he be jealous when he knows that the wedding is finished and the marriage is off to a good start?

'That's why my cup is running over. This is the assigned moment for him to move into the center, while I slip off to the sidelines.

'The One who comes from above is head and shoulders over other messengers from God. The earthborn is earthbound and speaks earth language; the heavenborn is in a league of his own. He sets out the evidence of what he saw and heard in heaven. No one wants to deal with these facts. But anyone who examines this evidence will come to stake his life on this: that God himself is the truth.

'The One that God sent speaks God's words. And don't think he rations out the Spirit in bits and pieces. The Father loves the Son extravagantly. He turned everything over to him so he could give it away – a lavish distribution of gifts. That is why whoever accepts and trusts the Son gets in on everything, life complete and forever! And that is also why the person who avoids and distrusts the Son is in the dark and doesn't see life. All he experiences of God is darkness, and an angry darkness at that.'

The Woman at the Well

4 Jesus realized that the Pharisees were keeping count of the baptisms that he and John performed (although his disciples, not Jesus, did the actual baptizing). They had posted the score that Jesus was ahead, turning him and John into rivals in the eyes of the people. So Jesus left the Judean countryside and went back to Galilee.

To get there, he had to pass through Samaria. He came into Sychar, a Samaritan village that bordered the field Jacob had given his son Joseph. Jacob's well was still there. Jesus, worn out by the trip, sat down at the well. It was noon.

A woman, a Samaritan, came to draw water. Jesus said, 'Would you give me a drink of water?' (His disciples had gone to the village to buy food for lunch.)

The Samaritan woman, taken aback, asked, 'How come you, a Jew, are asking me, a Samaritan woman, for a drink?'

(Jews in those days wouldn't be caught dead talking to Samaritans.)

Jesus answered, 'If you knew the generosity of God and who I am, you would be asking *me* for a drink, and I would give you fresh, living water.'

The woman said, 'Sir, you don't even have a bucket to draw with, and this well is deep. So how are you going to get this "living water"? Are you a better man than our ancestor Jacob, who dug this well and drank from it, he and his sons and livestock, and passed it down to us?'

Jesus said, 'Everyone who drinks this water will get thirsty again and again. Anyone who drinks the water I give will never thirst – not ever. The water I give will be an artesian spring within, gushing fountains of endless life.'

The woman said, 'Sir, give me this water so I won't ever get thirsty, won't ever have to come back to this well again!'

He said, 'Go call your husband and then come back.'

'I have no husband,' she said.

'That's nicely put: "I have no husband." You've had five husbands, and the man you're living with now isn't even your husband. You spoke the truth there, sure enough.'

'Oh, so you're a prophet! Well, tell me this: Our ancestors worshiped God at this mountain, but you Jews insist that Jerusalem is the only place for worship, right?'

'Believe me, woman, the time is coming when you Samaritans will worship the Father neither here at this mountain nor there in Jerusalem. You worship guessing in the dark; we Jews worship in the clear light of day. God's way of salvation is made available through the Jews. But the time is coming – it has, in fact, come – when what you're called will not matter and where you go to worship will not matter.

'It's who you are and the way you live that count before God. Your worship must engage your spirit in the pursuit of truth. That's the kind of people the Father is out looking for: those who are simply and honestly *themselves* before him in their worship. God is sheer being itself – Spirit. Those who worship him must do it out of their very being, their spirits, their true selves, in adoration.'

The woman said, 'I don't know about that. I do know that the Messiah is coming. When he arrives, we'll get the whole story.'

'I am he,' said Jesus. 'You don't have to wait any longer or look any further.'

Just then his disciples came back. They were shocked. They couldn't believe he was talking with that kind of a woman. No one said what they were all thinking, but their faces showed it.

The woman took the hint and left. In her confusion she left her water pot. Back in the village she told the people, 'Come see a man who knew all about the things I did, who knows me inside and out. Do you think this could be the Messiah?' And they went out to see for themselves.

It's Harvest Time

In the meantime, the disciples pressed him, 'Rabbi, eat. Aren't you going to eat?'

He told them, 'I have food to eat you know nothing about.'

The disciples were puzzled. 'Who could have brought him food?'

Jesus said, 'The food that keeps me going is that I do the will of the One who sent me, finishing the work he started.

As you look around right now, wouldn't you say that in about four months it will be time to harvest? Well, I'm telling you to open your eyes and take a good look at what's right in front of you. These Samaritan fields are ripe. It's harvest time!

'The Harvester isn't waiting. He's taking his pay, gathering in this grain that's ripe for eternal life. Now the Sower is arm in arm with the Harvester, triumphant. That's the truth of the saying, "This one sows, that one harvests." I sent you to harvest a field you never worked. Without lifting a finger, you have walked in on a field worked long and hard by others.'

Many of the Samaritans from that village committed themselves to him because of the woman's witness: 'He knew all about the things I did. He knows me inside and out!' They asked him to stay on, so Jesus stayed two days. A lot more people entrusted their lives to him when they heard what he had to say. They said to the woman, 'We're no longer taking this on your say-so. We've heard it for ourselves and know it for sure. He's the Savior of the world!'

After the two days he left for Galilee. Now, Jesus knew well from experience that a prophet is not respected in the place where he grew up. So when he arrived in Galilee, the Galileans welcomed him, but only because they were impressed with what he had done in Jerusalem during the Passover Feast, not that they really had a clue about who he was or what he was up to.

Now he was back in Cana of Galilee, the place where he made the water into wine. Meanwhile in Capernaum, there was a certain official from the king's court whose son was sick. When he heard that Jesus had come from Judea to

Galilee, he went and asked that he come down and heal his son, who was on the brink of death. Jesus put him off: 'Unless you people are dazzled by a miracle, you refuse to believe.'

But the court official wouldn't be put off. 'Come down! It's life or death for my son.'

Jesus simply replied, 'Go home. Your son lives.'

The man believed the bare word Jesus spoke and headed home. On his way back, his servants intercepted him and announced, 'Your son lives!'

He asked them what time he began to get better. They said, 'The fever broke yesterday afternoon at one o'clock.' The father knew that that was the very moment Jesus had said, 'Your son lives.'

That clinched it. Not only he but his entire household believed. This was now the second sign Jesus gave after having come from Judea into Galilee.

Even on the Sabbath

5 Soon another Feast came around and Jesus was back in Jerusalem. Near the Sheep Gate in Jerusalem there was a pool, in Hebrew called *Bethesda*, with five alcoves. Hundreds of sick people – blind, crippled, paralyzed – were in these alcoves. One man had been an invalid there for thirty-eight years. When Jesus saw him stretched out by the pool and knew how long he had been there, he said, 'Do you want to get well?'

The sick man said, 'Sir, when the water is stirred, I don't have anybody to put me in the pool. By the time I get there, somebody else is already in.'

Jesus said, 'Get up, take your bedroll, start walking.' The man was healed on the spot. He picked up his bedroll and walked off.

That day happened to be the Sabbath. The Jews stopped the healed man and said, 'It's the Sabbath. You can't carry your bedroll around. It's against the rules.'

But he told them, 'The man who made me well told me to. He said, "Take your bedroll and start walking."'

They asked, 'Who gave you the order to take it up and start walking?' But the healed man didn't know, for Jesus had slipped away into the crowd.

A little later Jesus found him in the Temple and said, 'You look wonderful! You're well! Don't return to a sinning life or something worse might happen.'

The man went back and told the Jews that it was Jesus who had made him well. That is why the Jews were out to get Jesus – because he did this kind of thing on the Sabbath.

But Jesus defended himself. 'My Father is working straight through, even on the Sabbath. So am I.'

That really set them off. The Jews were now not only out to expose him; they were out to *kill* him. Not only was he breaking the Sabbath, but he was calling God his own Father, putting himself on a level with God.

What the Father does, the Son Does

So Jesus explained himself at length. 'I'm telling you this straight. The Son can't independently do a thing, only what he sees the Father doing. What the Father does, the Son does. The Father loves the Son and includes him in everything he is doing.

'But you haven't seen the half of it yet, for in the same way that the Father raises the dead and creates life, so does the Son. The Son gives life to anyone he chooses. Neither he nor the Father shuts anyone out. The Father handed all authority to judge over to the Son so that the Son will be honored equally with the Father. Anyone who dishonors the Son, dishonors the Father, for it was the Father's decision to put the Son in the place of honor.

'It's urgent that you listen carefully to this: Anyone here who believes what I am saying right now and aligns himself with the Father, who has in fact put me in charge, has at this very moment the real, lasting life and is no longer condemned to be an outsider. This person has taken a giant step from the world of the dead to the world of the living.

'It's urgent that you get this right: The time has arrived – I mean right now! – when dead men and women will hear the voice of the Son of God and, hearing, will come alive. Just as the Father has life in himself, he has conferred on the Son life in himself. And he has given him the authority, simply because he is the Son of Man, to decide and carry out matters of Judgment.

'Don't act so surprised at all this. The time is coming when everyone dead and buried will hear his voice. Those who have lived the right way will walk out into a resurrection Life; those who have lived the wrong way, into a resurrection Judgment.

'I can't do a solitary thing on my own: I listen, then I decide. You can trust my decision because I'm not out to get my own way but only to carry out orders. If I were simply speaking on my own account, it would be an empty, self-serving witness. But an independent witness confirms me, the most reliable Witness of all. Furthermore, you all saw and heard John, and he gave expert and reliable testimony about me, didn't he?

'But my purpose is not to get your vote, and not to appeal to mere human testimony. I'm speaking to you this way so that you will be saved. John was a torch, blazing and bright, and you were glad enough to dance for an hour or so in his bright light. But the witness that really confirms me far exceeds John's witness. It's the work the Father gave me to complete. These very tasks, as I go about completing them, confirm that the Father, in fact, sent me. The Father who sent me, confirmed me. And you missed it. You never heard his voice, you never saw his appearance. There is nothing left in your memory of his Message because you do not take his Messenger seriously.'

'You have your heads in your Bibles constantly because you think you'll find eternal life there. But you miss the forest for the trees. These Scriptures are all about *me*! And here I am, standing right before you, and you aren't willing to receive from me the life you say you want.

'I'm not interested in crowd approval. And do you know why? Because I know you and your crowds. I know that love, especially God's love, is not on your working agenda. I came with the authority of my Father, and you either dismiss me or avoid me. If another came, acting self-important, you would welcome him with open arms. How do you expect to get anywhere with God when you spend all your time jockeying for position with each other, ranking your rivals and ignoring God?

'But don't think I'm going to accuse you before my Father. Moses, in whom you put so much stock, is your accuser. If you believed, really believed, what Moses said, you would believe me. He wrote of me. If you won't take seriously what *he* wrote, how can I expect you to take seriously what *I* speak?'

Bread and Fish for All

6 After this, Jesus went across the Sea of Galilee (some call it Tiberias). A huge crowd followed him, attracted by the miracles they had seen him do among the sick. When he got to the other side, he climbed a hill and sat down, surrounded by his disciples. It was nearly time for the Feast of Passover, kept annually by the Jews.

When Jesus looked out and saw that a large crowd had arrived, he said to Philip, 'Where can we buy bread to feed these people?' He said this to stretch Philip's faith. He already knew what he was going to do.

Philip answered, 'Two hundred silver pieces wouldn't be enough to buy bread for each person to get a piece.'

One of the disciples – it was Andrew, brother to Simon Peter – said, 'There's a little boy here who has five barley loaves and two fish. But that's a drop in the bucket for a crowd like this.'

Jesus said, 'Make the people sit down.' There was a nice carpet of green grass in this place. They sat down, about five thousand of them. Then Jesus took the bread and, having given thanks, gave it to those who were seated. He did the same with the fish. All ate as much as they wanted.

When the people had eaten their fill, he said to his disciples, 'Gather the leftovers so nothing is wasted.' They went to work and filled twelve large baskets with leftovers from the five barley loaves.

The people realized that God was at work among them in what Jesus had just done. They said, 'This is the Prophet for sure, God's Prophet right here in Galilee!' Jesus saw that in their enthusiasm, they were about to grab him and make him king, so he slipped off and went back up the mountain to be by himself.

In the evening his disciples went down to the sea, got in the boat, and headed back across the water to Capernaum. It had grown quite dark and Jesus had not yet returned. A huge wind blew up, churning the sea. They were maybe three or four miles out when they saw Jesus walking on the sea, quite near the boat. They were scared senseless, but he reassured them, 'It's me. It's all right. Don't be afraid.' So they took him on board. In no time they reached land – the exact spot they were headed to.

The next day the crowd that was left behind realized that there had been only one boat, and that Jesus had not gotten into it with his disciples. They had seen them go off without him. By now boats from Tiberias had pulled up near where they had eaten the bread blessed by the Master. So when the crowd realized he was gone and wasn't coming back, they piled into the Tiberias boats and headed for Capernaum, looking for Jesus.

When they found him back across the sea, they said, 'Rabbi, when did you get here?'

Jesus answered, 'You've come looking for me not because you saw God in my actions but because I fed you, filled your stomachs – and for free.'

The Bread of Life

'Don't waste your energy striving for perishable food like that. Work for the food that sticks with you, food that nourishes your lasting life, food the Son of Man provides.

He and what he does are guaranteed by God the Father to last.'

To that they said, 'Well, what do we do then to get in on God's works?'

Jesus said, 'Throw your lot in with the One that God has sent. That kind of a commitment gets you in on God's works.'

They waffled: 'Why don't you give us a clue about who you are, just a hint of what's going on? When we see what's up, we'll commit ourselves. Show us what you can do. Moses fed our ancestors with bread in the desert. It says so in the Scriptures: "He gave them bread from heaven to eat." '

Jesus responded, 'The real significance of that Scripture is not that Moses gave you bread from heaven but that my Father is right now offering you bread from heaven, the *real* bread. The Bread of God came down out of heaven and is giving life to the world.'

They jumped at that: 'Master, give us this bread, now and forever!'

Jesus said, 'I am the Bread of Life. The person who aligns with me hungers no more and thirsts no more, ever. I have told you this explicitly because even though you have seen me in action, you don't really believe me. Every person the Father gives me eventually comes running to me. And once that person is with me, I hold on and don't let go. I came down from heaven not to follow my own whim but to accomplish the will of the One who sent me.

'This, in a nutshell, is that will: that everything handed over to me by the Father be completed – not a single detail missed – and at the wrap-up of time I have everything and everyone put together, upright and whole. This is what my Father wants: that anyone who sees the Son and trusts who he is and what he does and then aligns with him will enter *real* life, *eternal* life. My part is to put them on their feet alive and whole at the completion of time.'

At this, because he said 'I am the Bread that came down from heaven,' the Jews started arguing over him: 'Isn't this the son of Joseph? Don't we know his father? Don't we know his mother? How can he now say "I came down out of heaven" and expect anyone to believe him?'

Jesus said, 'Don't bicker among yourselves over me. You're not in charge here. The Father who sent me is in charge. He draws people to me – that's the only way you'll ever come. Only then do I do my work, putting people together, setting them on their feet, ready for the End. This is what the prophets meant when they wrote, "And then they will all be personally taught by God." Anyone who has spent any time at all listening to the Father, really listening and therefore learning, comes to me to be taught personally – to see it with his own eyes, hear it with his own ears, from me, since I have it firsthand from the Father. No one has seen the Father except the One who has his Being alongside the Father – and you can *see me*.

'I'm telling you the most solemn and sober truth now: Whoever believes in me has real life, eternal life. I am the Bread of Life. Your ancestors ate the manna bread in the desert and died. But now here is Bread that truly comes down out of heaven. Anyone eating this Bread will not die, ever. I am the Bread – living Bread! – who came down out of heaven. Anyone who eats this Bread will live – and for-ever! The Bread that I present to the world so that it can eat and live is myself, this flesh-and-blood self.'

At this, the Jews started fighting among themselves: 'How can this man serve up his flesh for a meal?'

But Jesus didn't give an inch. 'Only insofar as you eat and drink flesh and blood, the flesh and blood of the Son of

Man, do you have life within you. The one who brings a hearty appetite to this eating and drinking has eternal life and will be fit and ready for the Final Day. My flesh is real food and my blood is real drink. By eating my flesh and drinking my blood you enter into me and I into you. In the same way that the fully alive Father sent me here and I live because of him, so the one who makes a meal of me lives because of me. This is the Bread from heaven. Your ancestors ate bread, and later died. Whoever eats this Bread will live always.'

He said these things while teaching in the meeting place in Capernaum.

Just Like Jesus

Max Lucado

Do you ever feel you can't change your character? Gifted communicator Max Lucado believes that God loves you the way you are, but he refuses to leave you there. He wants you to have a heart like his. He wants you to be just like Jesus.

ISBN: 0-8499-3717-5

Price: £6.99

1

A Heart Like His

What if, for one day, Jesus were to become you?

What if, for twenty-four hours, Jesus wakes up in your bed, walks in your shoes, lives in your house, assumes your schedule? Your boss becomes his boss, your mother becomes his mother, your pains become his pains? With one exception, nothing about your life changes. Your health doesn't change. Your circumstances don't change. Your schedule isn't altered. Your problems aren't solved. Only one change occurs.

What if, for one day and one night, Jesus lives your life with his heart? Your heart gets the day off, and your life is led by the heart of Christ. His priorities govern your actions. His passions drive your decisions. His love directs your behavior.

What would you be like? Would people notice a change? Your family – would they see something new? Your coworkers – would they sense a difference? What about the less fortunate? Would you treat them the same? And your friends? Would they detect more joy? How about your enemies? Would they receive more mercy from Christ's heart than from yours?

And you? How would you feel? What alterations would this transplant have on your stress level? Your mood swings? Your temper? Would you sleep better? Would you see sunsets differently? Death differently? Taxes differently? Any chance you'd need fewer aspirin or sedatives? How about your reaction to traffic delays? (Ouch, that touched a nerve.) Would you still dread what you are dreading? Better yet, would you still do what you are doing?

Would you still do what you had planned to do for the next twenty-four hours? Pause and think about your schedule. Obligations. Engagements. Outings. Appointments. With Jesus taking over your heart, would anything change?

Keep working on this for a moment. Adjust the lens of your imagination until you have a clear picture of Jesus leading your life, then snap the shutter and frame the image. What you see is what God wants. He wants you to 'think and act like Christ Jesus' (Phil. 2:5).

God's plan for you is nothing short of a new heart. If you were a car, God would want control of your engine. If you were a computer, God would claim the software and the hard drive. If you were an airplane, he'd take his seat in the cockpit. But you are a person, so God wants to change your heart.

'But you were taught to be made new in your hearts, to become a new person. That new person is made to be like God – made to be truly good and holy' (Eph. 4:23–24).

God wants you to be just like Jesus. He wants you to have a heart like his.

I'm going to risk something here. It's dangerous to sum up grand truths in one statement, but I'm going to try. If a sentence or two could capture God's desire for each of us, it might read like this:

God loves you just the way you are, but he refuses to leave you that way. He wants you to be just like Jesus.

God loves you just the way you are. If you think his love for you would be stronger if your faith were, you are wrong. If you think his love would be deeper if your thoughts were, wrong again. Don't confuse God's love with the love of people. The love of people often increases with performance and decreases with mistakes. Not so with God's love. He loves you right where you are. To quote my wife's favorite author:

> God's love never ceases. Never. Though we spurn him. Ignore him. Reject him. Despite him. Disobey him. He will not change. Our evil cannot diminish his love. Our goodness cannot increase it. Our faith does not earn it anymore than our stupidity jeopardizes it. God doesn't love us less if we fail or more if we succeed. God's love never ceases.[1]

God loves you just the way you are, but he refuses to leave you that way.

When my daughter Jenna was a toddler, I used to take her to a park not far from our apartment. One day as she was playing in a sandbox, an ice-cream salesman approached us. I purchased her a treat, and when I turned to give it to her, I saw her mouth was full of sand. Where I intended to put a delicacy, she had put dirt.

Did I love her with dirt in her mouth? Absolutely. Was she any less my daughter with dirt in her mouth? Of course not. Was I going to allow her to keep the dirt in her mouth? No way. I loved her right where she was, but I refused to leave her there. I carried her over to the water fountain and washed out her mouth. Why? Because I love her.

God does the same for us. He holds us over the fountain. 'Spit out the dirt, honey,' our Father urges. 'I've got something better for you.' And so he cleanses us of filth: immorality, dishonesty, prejudice, bitterness, greed. We don't enjoy the cleansing; sometimes we even opt for the dirt over the ice-cream. 'I can eat dirt if I want to!' we pout and proclaim. Which is true – we can. But if we do, the loss is ours. God has a better offer. He wants us to be just like Jesus.

Isn't that good news? You aren't stuck with today's personality. You aren't condemned to 'grumpydom.' You are tweakable. Even if you've worried each day of your life, you needn't worry the rest of your life. So what if you were born a bigot? You don't have to die one.

Where did we get the idea we can't change? From whence come statements such as, 'It's just my nature to worry,' or, 'I'll always be pessimistic. I'm just that way,' or, 'I have a bad temper. I can't help the way I react'? Who says? Would we make similar statements about our bodies? 'It's just my nature to have a broken leg. I can't do anything about it.' Of course not. If our bodies malfunction, we seek help. Shouldn't we do the same with our hearts? Shouldn't we seek aid for our sour attitudes? Can't we request treatment for our selfish tirades? Of course we can. Jesus can change our hearts. He wants us to have a heart like his.

Can you imagine a better offer?

The heart of Christ

The heart of Jesus was pure. The Savior was adored by thousands, yet content to live a simple life. He was cared for by women (Luke 8:1–3), yet never accused of lustful thoughts; scorned by his own creation, but willing to forgive them before they even requested his mercy. Peter, who traveled with Jesus for three and a half years, described him as a 'lamb, unblemished and spotless' (1 Pet. 1:19). After spending the same amount of time with Jesus, John concluded, 'And in him is no sin' (1 John 3:5).

Jesus' heart was peaceful. The disciples fretted over the need to feed the thousands, but not Jesus. He thanked God for the problem. The disciples shouted for fear in the storm, but not Jesus. He slept through it. Peter drew his sword to fight the soldiers, but not Jesus. He lifted his hand to heal. His heart was at peace. When his disciples abandoned him, did he pout and go home? When Peter denied him, did Jesus lose his temper? When the soldiers spit in his face, did he breathe fire in theirs? Far from it. He was at peace. He forgive them. He refused to be guided by vengeance.

He also refused to be guided by anything other than his high call. His heart was purposeful. Most lives aim at nothing in particular and achieve it. Jesus aimed at one goal– to save humanity from its sin. He could summarize his life with one sentence: 'The Son of man came to seek and to save the lost' (Luke 19:10 RSV). Jesus was so focused on his task that he knew when to say, 'My time has not yet come' (John 2:4) and when to say, 'It is finished' (John 19:30). But he was not so focused on his goal that he was unpleasant.

Quite the contrary. How pleasant were his thoughts! Children couldn't resist Jesus. He could find beauty in lilies, joy in worship, and possibilities in problems. He would spend days with multitudes of sick people and still feel sorry for them. He spent over three decades wading through the muck and mire of our sin yet still saw enough beauty in us to die for our mistakes.

But the crowning attribute of Christ was this: his heart was spiritual. His thoughts reflected his intimate relationship with the Father. 'I am in the Father and the Father is in me,' he stated (John 14:11). His first recorded sermon begins with the words, 'The Spirit of the Lord is upon Me' (Luke 4:18 NASB). He was 'led by the Spirit' (Matt. 4:1 NIV) and 'full of the Holy Spirit' (Luke 4:1 NIV). He returned from the desert 'in the power of the Spirit' (Luke 4:14 NIV).

Jesus took his instructions from God. It was his habit to go to worship (Luke 4:16). It was his practice to memorize scripture (Luke 4:4). Luke says Jesus 'often slipped away to be alone so he could pray' (Luke 5:16). His times of prayer guided him. He once returned from prayer and announced it was time to move to another city (Mark 1:38). Another time of prayer resulted in the selection of the disciples (Luke 6:12–13). Jesus was led by an unseen hand. 'The Son does whatever the Father does' (John 5:19). In the same chapter he stated, 'I can do nothing alone. I judge only the way I am told' (John 5:30).

The heart of Jesus was spiritual.

The heart of humanity

Our hearts seem so far from his. He is pure; we are greedy. He is peaceful; we are hassled. He is purposeful; we are distracted. He is pleasant; we are cranky. He is spiritual; we are earth-bound. The distance between our hearts and his seems so immense. How could we ever hope to have the heart of Jesus?

Ready for a surprise? You already do. You already have the heart of Christ. Why are you looking at me that way? Would I kid you? If you are in Christ, you already have the heart of Christ. One of the supreme yet unrealized promises of God is simply this: if you have given your life to Jesus, Jesus has given himself to you. He has made your heart his home. It would be hard to say it more succinctly than Paul does: 'Christ lives in me' (Gal. 2:20 MSG).

At the risk of repeating myself, let me repeat myself. If you have given your life to Jesus, Jesus has given himself to you. He has moved in and unpacked his bags and is ready to change you 'into his likeness from one degree of glory to another' (2 Cor. 3:18 RSV). Paul explains it with these words: 'Strange as it seems, we Christians actually do have within us a portion of the very thoughts and mind of Christ' (1 Cor. 2:16 TLB).

Strange is the word! If I have the mind of Jesus, why do I still think so much like me? If I have the heart of Christ, why do I still have the hang-ups of Max? If Jesus dwells within me, why do I still hate traffic jams?

Part of the answer is illustrated in a story about a lady who had a small house on the seashore of Ireland at the turn of the century. She was quite wealthy but also quite frugal. The people were surprised, then, when she decided to be among the first to have electricity in her home.

Several weeks after the installation, a meter reader appeared at her door. He asked if her electricity was working well, and she assured him it was. 'I'm wondering if you can explain something to me,' he said. 'Your meter shows scarcely any usage. Are you using your power?'

'Certainly,' she answered. 'Each evening when the sun sets, I turn on my lights just long enough to light my candles; then I turn them off.'[2]

She's tapped into the power but doesn't use it. Her house is connected but not altered. Don't we make the same mistake? We, too – with our souls saved but our hearts unchanged – are connected but not altered. Trusting Christ for salvation but resisting transformation. We occasionally flip the switch, but most of the time we settle for shadows.

What would happen if we left the light on? What would happen if we not only flipped the switch but lived in the light? What changes would occur if we set about the task of dwelling in the radiance of Christ?

No doubt about it: God has ambitious plans for us. The same one who saved your soul longs to remake your heart: His plan is nothing short of a total transformation: 'He decided from the outset to shape the lives of those who love him along the same lines as the life of his Son' (Rom. 8:29MSG).

'You have begun to live the new life, in which you are being made new and are becoming like the One who made you. This new life brings you the true knowledge of God' (Col. 3:10).

God is willing to change us into the likeness of the Savior. Shall we accept his offer? Here is my suggestion. Let's imagine what it means to be just like Jesus. Let's look long into the heart of Christ. Let's spend some chapters considering his compassion, reflecting upon his intimacy with the Father, admiring his focus, pondering his endurance. How did he forgive? When did he pray? What made him so pleasant? Why didn't he give up? Let's 'fix our eyes on Jesus' (Heb. 12:2 NIV). Perhaps in seeing him, we will see what we can become.

Mere Christianity

C. S. Lewis

Lewis' legendary brilliance remains strikingly fresh for the modern readers. In this famous collection, he set out simply to 'explain and defend the belief that has been common to nearly all Christians at all times'. He has the unique power for making theology an attractive, exciting and fascinating quest.

ISBN: 0-00-6280544

Price: £7.99

First published in 1952 by Geoffrey Bles,
by Fontana Books in 1995, and by Fount Paperbacks in 1977
This edition 1997
Fount Paperbacks is an imprint of HarperCollins*Religious*,
Part of HarperCollins*Publishers*,
77–85 Fulham Palace Road, London W6 8JB

The Law of Human Nature

Every one has heard people quarrelling. Sometimes it sounds funny and sometimes it sounds merely unpleasant; but however it sounds, I believe we can learn something very important from listening to the kind of things they say. They say things like this: 'How'd you like it if anyone did the same to you?' – 'That's my seat, I was there first' – 'Leave him alone, he isn't doing you any harm' – 'Why should you shove in first?' – 'Give me a bit of your orange, I gave you a bit of mine' – 'Come on, you promised.' People say things like that every day, educated people as well as uneducated, and children as well as grown-ups.

Now what interests me about all these remarks is that the man who makes them is not merely saying that the other man's behaviour does not happen to please him. He is appealing to some kind of standard of behaviour which he expects the other man to know about. And the other man very seldom replies: 'To hell with your standard.' Nearly always he tries to make out that what he has been doing does not really go against the standard, or that if it does there is some special excuse. He pretends there is some special reason in this particular case why the person who took the seat first should not keep it, or that things were quite different when he was given the bit of orange, or that something has turned up which lets him off keeping his promise. It looks, in fact, very much as if both parties had in mind some kind of Law or Rule of fair play or decent behaviour or morality or whatever you like to call it, about which they really agreed. And they have. If they had not, they might, of course, fight like animals, but they could not quarrel in the human sense of the word. Quarrelling means trying to show that the other man is in the wrong. And there would be no sense in trying to do that unless you and he had some sort of agreement as to what Right and Wrong are; just as there would be no sense in saying that a footballer had committed a foul unless there was some agreement about the rules of football.

Now this Law or Rule about Right and Wrong used to be called the Law of Nature. Nowadays, when we talk of the 'laws of nature' we usually mean things like gravitation, or heredity, or the laws of chemistry. But when the older thinkers called the Law of Right and Wrong 'the Law of Nature', they really meant the Law of Human Nature. The idea was that, just as all bodies are governed by the law of gravitation, and organisms by biological laws, so the creature called man also had his law – with this great difference, that a body could not choose whether it obeyed the law of gravitation or not, but a man could choose either to obey the Law of Human Nature or to disobey it.

We may put this in another way. Each man is at every moment subjected to several different sets of law but there is only one of these which he is free to disobey. As a body, he is subjected to gravitation and cannot disobey it; if you leave him unsupported in mid-air, he has no more choice about falling than a stone has. As an organism, he is subjected to various biological laws which he cannot disobey any more than an animal can. That is, he cannot disobey those laws which he shares with other things; but the law which is peculiar to his human nature, the law he does not share with animals or vegetables or inorganic things, is the one he can disobey if he chooses.

This law was called the Law of Nature because people thought that every one knew it by nature and did not need to be taught it. They did not mean, of course, that you might not find an odd individual here and there who did not know it, just as you find a few people who are colour-blind or have no ear for a tune. But taking the race as a whole, they thought that the human idea of decent behaviour was obvious to every one. And I believe they were right. If they were not, then all the things we said about the war were nonsense. What was the sense in saying the enemy were in the wrong unless Right is a real thing which the Nazis at bottom knew as well as we did and ought to have practised? If they had had no notion of what we mean by right, then, though we might still have had to fight them, we could no more have blamed them for that than for the colour of their hair.

I know that some people say the idea of a Law of Nature or decent behaviour known to all men is unsound, because different civilisations and different ages have had quite different moralities.

But this is not true. There have been differences between their moralities, but these have never amounted to anything like a total difference. If anyone will take the trouble to compare the moral teaching of, say, the ancient Egyptians, Babylonians, Hindus, Chinese, Greeks and Romans, what will really strike him will be how very like they are to each other and to our own. Some of the evidence for this I have put together in the appendix of

another book called *The Abolition of Man*; but for our present purpose I need only ask the reader to think what a
totally different morality would mean. Think of a country
where people were admired for running away in battle, or
where a man felt proud of double-crossing all the people
who had been kindest to him. You might just as well try to
imagine a country where two and two made five. Men
have differed as regards what people you ought to be
unselfish to – whether it was only your own family, or your
fellow countrymen, or every one. But they have always
agreed that you ought not to put yourself first. Selfishness
has never been admired. Men have differed as to whether
you should have one wife or four. But they have always
agreed that you must not simply have any woman you
liked.

But the most remarkable thing is this. Whenever you
find a man who says he does not believe in a real Right and
Wrong, you will find the same man going back on this a
moment later. He may break his promise to you, but if you
try breaking one to him he will be complaining 'It's not
fair' before you can say Jack Robinson. A nation may say
treaties don't matter; but then, next minute, they spoil their
case by saying that the particular treaty they want to break
was an unfair one. But if treaties do not matter, and if there
is no such thing as Right and Wrong – in other words, if
there is no Law of Nature – what is the difference between
a fair treaty and an unfair one? Have they not let the cat out
of the bag and shown that, whatever they say, they really
know the Law of Nature just like anyone else?

It seems, then, we are forced to believe in a real Right
and Wrong. People may be sometimes mistaken about
them, just as people sometimes get their sums wrong; but
they are not a matter of mere taste and opinion any more

than the multiplication table. Now if we are agreed about that, I go on to my next point, which is this. None of us are really keeping the Law of Nature. If there are any exceptions among you, I apologise to them. They had much better read some other book, for nothing I am going to say concerns them. And now, turning to the ordinary human beings who are left:

I hope you will not misunderstand what I am going to say. I am not preaching, and Heaven knows I do not pretend to be better than anyone else. I am only trying to call attention to a fact; the fact that this year, or this month, or, more likely, this very day, we have failed to practise ourselves the kind of behaviour we expect from other people. There may be all sorts of excuses for us. That time you were so unfair to the children was when you were very tired. That slightly shady business about the money – the one you have almost forgotten – came when you were very hard-up. And what you promised to do for old So-and-so and have never done – well, you never would have promised if you had known how frightfully busy you were going to be. And as for your behaviour to your wife (or husband) or sister (or brother) if I knew how irritating they could be, I would not wonder at it – and who the dickens am I, anyway? I am just the same. That is to say, I do not succeed in keeping the Law of Nature very well, and the moment anyone tells me I am not keeping it, there starts up in my mind a string of excuses as long as your arm. The question at the moment is not whether they are good excuses. The point is that they are one more proof of how deeply, whether we like it or not, we believe in the Law of Nature. If we do not believe in decent behaviour, why should we be so anxious to make excuses for not having behaved decently? The truth is, we believe in decency so much – we feel the Rule of Law pressing on us so – that we cannot bear to face the fact that we are breaking it, and consequently we try to shift the responsibility. For you notice that it is only for our bad behaviour that we find all these explanations. It is only our bad temper that we put down to being tired or worried or hungry; we put our good temper down to ourselves.

These, then, are the two points I wanted to make. First, that human beings, all over the earth, have this curious idea that they ought to behave in a certain way, and cannot really get rid of it. Secondly, that they do not in fact behave in that way. They know the Law of Nature; they break it. These two facts are the foundation of all clear thinking about ourselves and the universe we live in.

2

Some Objections

If they are the foundation, I had better stop to make that foundation firm before I go on. Some of the letters I have had show that a good many people find it difficult to understand just what this Law of Human Nature, or Moral Law, or Rule of Decent Behaviour is.

For example, some people wrote to me saying, 'Isn't what you call the Moral Law simply our herd instinct and hasn't it been developed just like all our other instincts?' Now I do not deny that we may have a herd instinct: but that is not what I mean by the Moral Law. We all know what it feels like to be prompted by instinct – by mother love, or sexual instinct, or the instinct for food. It means that you feel a strong want or desire to act in a certain way. And, of course, we sometimes do feel just that sort of desire to help another person: and no doubt that desire is due to the herd instinct. But feeling a desire to help is quite different from feeling that you ought to help whether you want to or not. Supposing you hear a cry for help from a man in danger. You will probably feel two desires – one a desire to give help (due to your herd instinct), the other a desire to keep out of danger (due to the instinct for self-preservation). But you will find inside you, in addition to these two impulses, a third thing which tells you that you ought to follow the impulse to help, and suppress the impulse to run away. Now this thing that judges between two instincts, that decides which should be encouraged, cannot itself be either of them. You might as well say that the sheet of music which tells you, at a given moment, to play one note on the piano and not another, is itself one of the notes on the keyboard. The Moral Law tells us the tune we have to play: our instincts are merely the keys.

Another way of seeing that the Moral Law is not simply one of our instincts is this. If two instincts are in conflict, and there is nothing in a creature's mind except those two instincts, obviously the stronger of the two must win. But at those moments when we are most conscious of the Moral Law, it usually seems to be telling us to side with the weaker of the two impulses. You probably *want* to be safe much more than you want to help the man who is drowning: but the Moral Law tells you to help him all the same. And surely it often tells us to try to make the right impulse stronger than it naturally is? I mean, we often feel it our duty to stimulate the herd instinct, by waking up our imaginations and arousing our pity and so on, so as to get up enough steam for doing the right thing. But clearly we are not acting *from* instinct when we set about making an instinct stronger than it is. The thing that says to you, 'Your herd instinct is asleep. Wake it up,' cannot itself *be* the herd instinct. The thing that tells you which note on the piano needs to be played louder cannot itself be that note.

Here is a third way of seeing it. If the Moral Law was one of our instincts, we ought to be able to point to some one impulse inside us which was always what we call 'good,' always in agreement with the rule of right behaviour. But you cannot. There is none of our impulses which the Moral

Law may not sometimes tell us to suppress, and none which it may not sometimes tell us to encourage. It is a mistake to think that some of our impulses – say mother love or patriotism – are good, and others, like sex or the fighting instinct, are bad. All we mean is that the occasions on which the fighting instinct or the sexual desire need to be restrained are rather more frequent that those for restraining mother love or patriotism. But there are situations in which it is the duty of a married man to encourage his sexual impulse and of a soldier to encourage his fighting instinct. There are also occasions on which a mother's love for her own children or a man's love for his own country have to be suppressed or they will lead to unfairness towards other people's children or countries. Strictly speaking, there are no such things as good and bad impulses. Think once again of a piano. It has not got two kinds of notes on it, the 'right' notes and the 'wrong' ones. Every single note is right at one time and wrong at another. The Moral Law is not any one instinct or set of instincts: it is something which makes a kind of tune (the tune we call goodness or right conduct) by directing the instincts.

By the way, the point is of great practical consequence. The most dangerous thing you can do is to take any one impulse of your own nature and set it up as the thing you ought to follow at all costs. There is not one of them which will not make us into devils if we set it up as an absolute guide. You might think love of humanity in general was safe, but it is not. If you leave out justice you will find yourself breaking agreements and faking evidence in trials 'for the sake of humanity', and become in the end a cruel and treacherous man.

Other people wrote to me saying, 'Isn't what you call the Moral Law just a social convention, something that is

put into us by education?' I think there is a misunderstanding here. The people who ask that question are usually
taking it for granted that if we have learned a thing from
parents and teachers, then that thing must be merely a
human invention. But, of course, that is not so. We all
learned the multiplication table at school. A child who
grew up alone on a desert island would not know it. But
surely it does not follows that the multiplication table is
simply a human convention, something human beings
have made up for themselves and might have made different if they had liked? I fully agree that we learn the Rule of
Decent Behaviour from parents and teachers, and friends
and books, as we learn everything else. But some of the
things we learn are mere conventions which might have
been different – we learn to keep to the left of the road, but
it might just as well have been the rule to keep to the right –
and others of them, like mathematics, are real truths. The
question is to which class the Law of Human Nature
belongs.

There are two reasons for saying it belongs to the same
class as mathematics. The first is, as I said in the first chapter,
that though there are differences between the moral ideas
of one time or country and those of another, the differences
are not really very great – not nearly so great as most people
imagine – and you can recognise the same law running
through them all: whereas mere conventions, like the rule
of the road or the kind of clothes people wear, may differ to
any extent. The other reason is this. When you think about
these differences between the morality of one people and
another, do you think that the morality of one people is
ever better or worse than that of another? Have any of the
changes been improvements? If not, then of course there
could never be any moral progress. Progress means not just

changing, but changing for the better. If no set of moral ideas were truer or better than any other, there would be no sense in preferring civilised morality to savage morality, or Christian morality to Nazi morality. In fact, of course, we all do believe that some moralities are better than others. We do believe that some of the people who tried to change the moral ideas of their own age were what we would call Reformers or Pioneers – people who understood morality better than their neighbours did. Very well then. The moment you say that one set of moral ideas can be better than another, you are, in fact, measuring them both by a standard, saying that one of them conforms to that standard more nearly than the other. But the standard that measures two things is something different from either. You are, in fact, comparing them both with some Real Morality, admitting that there is such a thing as a real Right, inde- pendent of what people think, and that some people's ideas get nearer to that real Right than others. Or put it this way. If your moral ideas can be truer, and those of the Nazis less true, there must be something – some Real Morality – for them to be true about. The reason why your idea of New York can be truer or less true than mine is that New York is a real place, existing quite apart from what either of us thinks. If when each of us said 'New York' each means merely 'The town I am imagining in my own head', how could one of us have truer ideas than the other? There would be no question of truth or falsehood at all. In the same way, if the Rule of Decent Behaviour meant simply 'whatever each nation happens to approve', there would be no sense in saying that any one nation had ever been more correct in its approval than any other; no sense in saying that the world could ever grow morally better or morally worse.

I conclude then, that though the difference between people's ideas of Decent Behaviour often make you suspect that there is no real natural Law of Behaviour at all, yet the things we are bound to think about these differences really prove just the opposite. But one word before I end. I have met people who exaggerate the differences, because they have not distinguished between differences of morality and differences of belief about facts. For example, one man said to me, 'Three hundred years ago people in England were putting witches to death. Was that what you call the Rule of Human Nature or Right Conduct?' But surely the reason we do not execute witches is that we do not believe there are such things. If we did – if we really thought that there were people going about who had sold themselves to the devil and received supernatural powers from him in return and were using these powers to kill their neighbours or drive them mad or bring bad weather – surely we would all agree that if anyone deserved the death penalty, then these filthy quislings did? There is no difference of moral principle here: the difference is simply about matter of fact. It may be a great advance in knowledge not to believe in witches: there is no moral advance in not executing them when you do not think they are there. You would not call a man humane for ceasing to set mousetraps if he did so because he believed there were no mice in the house.

What's So Amazing About Grace?

Philip Yancey

'The world thirsts for grace', says award winning author Philip Yancey. This brilliant book gives us a probing and impassioned look at the subject, true portraits of grace's life-changing power and challenges us to become living answers to a world that desperately wants to know, *What's So Amazing About Grace?*

ISBN: 0-310-21862-4

Price: £7.99

I know nothing, except what everyone knows —
if there when Grace dances, I should dance.
W. H. AUDEN

1

The Last Best Word

I told a story in my book *The Jesus I Never Knew*, a true
story that long afterward continued to haunt me. I heard it
from a friend who works with the down-and-out in
Chicago:

> A prostitute came to me in wretched straits, homeless, sick,
> unable to buy food for her two-year-old daughter. Through
> sobs and tears, she told me she had been renting out her
> daughter – two years old! – to men interested in kinky sex. She
> made more renting out her daughter for an hour than she
> could earn on her own in a night. She had to do it, she said, to
> support her own drug habit. I could hardly bear hearing her
> sordid story. For one thing, it made me legally liable – I'm
> required to report cases of child abuse. I had no idea what to
> say to this woman.
>
> At last I asked if she had ever thought of going to a church
> for help. I will never forget the look of pure, naive shock that
> crossed her face. 'Church!' she cried. 'Why would I ever go
> there? I was already feeling terrible about myself. They'd just
> make me feel worse.'

What struck me about my friend's story is that women
much like this prostitute fled toward Jesus, not away from

him. The worse a person felt about herself, the more likely she saw Jesus as a refuge. Has the church lost that gift? Evidently the down-and-out, who flocked to Jesus when he lived on earth, no longer feel welcome among his followers. What has happened?

The more I pondered this question, the more I felt drawn to one word as the key. All that follows uncoils from that one word.

As a writer, I play with words all day long. I toy with them, listen for their overtones, crack them open, and try to stuff my thoughts inside. I've found that words tend to spoil over the years, like old meat. Their meaning rots away. Consider the word 'charity,' for instance. When King James translators contemplated the highest form of love they settled on the word 'charity' to convey it. Nowadays we hear the scornful protest, 'I don't want your charity!'

Perhaps I keep circling back to *grace* because it is one grand theological word that has not spoiled. I call it 'the last best word' because every English usage I can find retains some of the glory of the original. Like a vast aquifer, the word underlies our proud civilization, reminding us that good things come not from our own efforts, rather by the grace of God. Even now, despite our secular drift, taproots still stretch toward grace. Listen to how we use the word.

Many people 'say grace' before meals, acknowledging daily bread as a gift from God. We are *grateful* for someone's kindness, *gratified* by good news, *congratulated* when successful, *gracious* in hosting friends. When a person's service pleases us, we leave a *gratuity*. In each of these uses I hear a pang of childlike delight in the undeserved.

A composer of music may add *grace notes* to the score. Though not essential to the melody – they are *gratuitous* –

these notes add a flourish whose presence would be missed. When I first attempt a piano sonata by Beethoven or Schubert I play it through a few times without the grace notes. The sonata carries along, but oh what a difference it makes when I am able to add in the grace notes, which season the piece like savory spices.

In England, some uses hint loudly at the word's theological source. British subjects address royalty as 'Your grace.' Students at Oxford and Cambridge may 'receive a grace' exempting them from certain academic requirements. Parliament declares an 'act of grace' to pardon a criminal.

New York publishers also suggest the theological meaning with their policy of *gracing*. If I sign up for twelve issues of a magazine, I may receive a few extra copies even after my subscription has expired. These are 'grace issues,' sent free of charge (or, *gratis*) to tempt me to resubscribe. Credit cards, rental car agencies, and mortgage companies likewise extend to customers an undeserved 'grace period.'

I also learn about a word from its opposite. Newspapers speak of communism's 'fall from grace,' a phrase similarly applied to Jimmy Swaggart, Richard Nixon, and O. J. Simpson. We insult a person by pointing out the dearth of grace: 'You *ingrate!*' we say, or worse, 'You're a *disgrace!*' A truly despicable person has no 'saving grace' about him. My favorite use of the root word *grace* occurs in the mellifluous phrase *persona non grata*: a person who offends the U.S. government by some act of treachery is officially proclaimed a 'person without grace.'

The many uses of the word in English convince me that *grace* is indeed amazing – truly our last best word. It contains the essence of the gospel as a drop of water can contain the image of the sun. The world thirsts for grace in ways it does not even recognize; little wonder the hymn 'Amazing

Grace' edged its way onto the Top Ten charts two hundred years after composition. For a society that seems adrift, without moorings, I know of no better place to drop an anchor of faith.

Like grace notes in music, though, the state of grace proves fleeting. The Berlin Wall falls in a night of euphoria; South African blacks queue up in long, exuberant lines to cast their first votes ever; Yitzhak Rabin and Yasser Arafat shake hands in the Rose Garden – for a moment, grace descends. And then Eastern Europe sullenly settles into the long task of rebuilding, South Africa tries to figure out how to run a country, Arafat dodges bullets and Rabin is felled by one. Like a dying star, grace dissipates in a final burst of pale light, and is then engulfed by the black hole of 'ungrace.'

'The great Christian revolutions,' said H. Richard Niebuhr, 'come not by the discovery of something that was not known before. They happen when somebody takes radically something that was always there.' Oddly, I sometimes find a shortage of grace within the church, an institution founded to proclaim, in Paul's phrase, 'the gospel of God's grace.'

Author Stephen Brown notes that a veterinarian can learn a lot about a dog owner he has never met just by observing the dog. What does the world learn about God by watching us his followers on earth? Trace the roots of *grace*, or *charis* in Greek, and you will find a verb that means 'I rejoice, I am glad.' In my experience, rejoicing and gladness are not the first images that come to mind when people think of the church. They think of holier-than-thous. They think of church as a place to go after you have cleaned up your act, not before. They think of morality, not grace. 'Church!' said the prostitute, 'Why would I ever go there? I was already feeling terrible about myself. They'd just make me feel worse.'

Such an attitude comes partly from a misconception, or bias, by outsiders. I have visited soup kitchens, homeless shelters, hospices, and prison ministries staffed by Christian volunteers generous with grace. And yet the prostitute's comment stings because she has found a weak spot in the church. Some of us seem so anxious about avoiding hell that we forget to celebrate our journey toward heaven. Others of us, rightly concerned about issues in a modern 'culture war,' neglect the church's mission as a haven of grace in his world of ungrace.

'Grace is everywhere,' said the dying priest in Georges Bernanos's novel *Diary of a Country Priest.* Yes, but how easily we pass by, deaf to the euphony.

I attended a Bible college. Years later, when I was sitting next to the president of that school on an airplane, he asked me to assess my education. 'Some good, some bad,' I replied. 'I met many godly people there. In fact, I met God there. Who can place a value on that? And yet I later realized that in four years I learned almost nothing about grace. It may be the most important word in the Bible, the heart of the gospel. How could I have missed it?'

I related our conversation in a subsequent chapel address and, in doing so, offended the faculty. Some suggested I not be invited back to speak. One gentle soul wrote to ask whether I should have phrased things differently. Shouldn't I have said that as a student I lacked the receptors to receive the grace that was all around me? Because I respect and love this man, I thought long and hard about his question. Ultimately, however, I concluded that I had experienced as much ungrace on the campus of a Bible college as I had anywhere else in life.

A counselor, David Seamands, summed up his career this way:

> Many years ago I was driven to the conclusion that the two
> major causes of most emotional problems among evangelical
> Christians are these: the failure to understand, receive, and live
> out God's unconditional grace and forgiveness; and the failure
> to give out that unconditional love, forgiveness, and grace to
> other people. . . . We read, we hear, we believe a good theol-
> ogy of grace. But that's not the way we live. The good news of
> the Gospel of grace has not penetrated the level of our
> emotions.

'The world can do almost anything as well as or better than the church,' says Gordon MacDonald. 'You need not be a Christian to build houses, feed the hungry, or heal the sick. There is only one thing the world cannot do. It cannot offer grace.' MacDonald has put his finger on the church's single most important contribution. Where else can the world go to find grace?

The Italian novelist Ignazio Silone wrote about a revo-lutionary hunted by the police. In order to hide him, his comrades dressed him in the garb of a priest and sent him to a remote village in the foothills of the Alps. Word got out, and soon a long line of peasants appeared at his door, full of stories of their sins and broken lives. The 'priest' protested and tried to turn them away, to no avail. He had no recourse but to sit and listen to the stories of people starving for grace.

I sense, in fact, that is why any person goes to church: out of hunger for grace. The book *Growing Up Fundamen-talist* tells of a reunion of students from a missionary acad-emy in Japan. 'With one or two exceptions, all had left the faith and come back,' one of the students reported. 'And those of us who had come back had one thing in common: we had all discovered grace. . . .'

As I look back on my own pilgrimage, marked by wanderings, detours, and dead ends, I see now that what pulled me along was my search for grace. I rejected the church for a time because I found so little grace there. I returned because I found grace nowhere else.

I have barely tasted of grace myself, have rendered less than I have received, and am in no wise an 'expert' on grace. These are, in fact, the very reasons that impel me to write. I want to know more, to understand more, to experience more grace. I dare not – and the danger is very real – write an ungracious book about grace. Accept then, here at the beginning, that I write as a pilgrim qualified only by my craving for grace.

Grace does not offer an easy subject for a writer. To borrow E. B. White's comment about humor, '[Grace] can be dissected, as a frog, but the thing dies in the process, and the innards are discouraging to any but the pure scientific mind.' I have just read a thirteen-page treatise on grace in the *New Catholic Encyclopedia*, which has cured me of any desire to dissect grace and display its innards. I do not want the thing to die. For this reason, I will rely more on stories than on syllogisms.

In sum, I would far rather convey grace than explain it.

PART I

How Sweet the Sound

2

Babette's Feast: A Story

Karen Blixen, Danish by birth, married a baron and spent the years 1914–31 managing a coffee plantation in British East Africa (her *Out of Africa* tells of these years). After a divorce she returned to Denmark and began writing in English under the pseudonym Isak Dinesen. One of her stories, 'Babette's Feast,' became a cult classic after being made into a movie in the 1980s.

Dinesen set her story in Norway, but the Danish film-makers changed the location to an impoverished fishing village on the coast of Denmark, a town of muddy streets and thatched-roof hovels. In this grim setting, a white-bearded Dean led a group of worshipers in an austere Lutheran sect.

What few worldly pleasures could tempt a peasant in Norre Vosburg, this sect renounced. All wore black. Their diet consisted of boiled cod and a gruel made from boiling bread in water fortified with a splash of ale. On the Sabbath, the group met together and sang songs about 'Jerusalem, my happy home, name ever dear to me.' They had fixed their compasses on the New Jerusalem, with life on earth tolerated as a way to get there.

The old Dean, a widower, had two teenage daughters: Martine, named for Martin Luther, and Philippa, named for Luther's disciple Philip Melanchthon. Villagers used to attend the church just to feast their eyes on these two, whose radiant beauty could not be suppressed despite the sisters' best efforts.

Martine caught the eye of a dashing young cavalry officer. When she successfully resisted his advances — after all, who would care for her aging father? — he rode away to marry instead a lady-in-waiting to Queen Sophia.

Philippa possessed not only beauty but also the voice of a nightingale. When she sang about Jerusalem, shimmering visions of the heavenly city seemed to appear. And so it happened that Philippa made the acquaintance of the most famous operatic singer of the day, the Frenchman Achille Papin, who was spending some time on the coast for his health. As he walked the dirt paths of a backwater town, Papin heard to his astonishment a voice worthy of the Grand Opera of Paris.

Allow me to teach you to sing properly, he urged Philippa, and all of France will fall at your feet. Royalty will line up to meet you, and you will ride in a horse-drawn carriage to dine at the magnificent Café Anglais. Flattered, Philippa consented to a few lessons, but only a few. Singing about love made her nervous, the flutterings she felt inside troubled her further, and when an aria from *Don Giovanni* ended with her being held in Papin's embrace, his lips brushing hers, she knew beyond doubt that these new pleasures must be renounced. Her father wrote a note declining all future lessons, and Achille Papin returned to Paris, as disconsolate as if he'd misplaced a winning lottery ticket.

Fifteen years passed, and much changed in the village. The two sisters, now middle-aged spinsters, had attempted to carry on the mission of their deceased father, but without his stern leadership the sect splintered badly. One Brother bore a grudge against another concerning some business matter. Rumors spread about a thirty-year-old sexual affair involving two of the members. A pair of old ladies had not spoken to each other for a decade. Although the sect still met on the Sabbath and sang the old hymns, only a handful bothered to attend, and the music had lost its luster. Despite all these problems, the Dean's two daughters remained faithful, organizing the services and boiling bread for the toothless elders of the village.

One night, a night too rainy for anyone to venture on the muddy streets, the sisters heard a heavy thump at the door. When they opened it, a woman collapsed in a swoon. They revived her only to find she spoke no Danish. She handed them a letter from Achille Papin. At the sight of his name Philippa's face flushed, and her hand trembled as she read the letter of introduction. The woman's name was Babette, and she had lost her husband and son during the civil war in France. Her life in danger, she had to flee, and Papin had found her passage on a ship in hopes that this village might show her mercy. 'Babette can cook,' the letter read.

The sisters had no money to pay Babette and felt dubious about employing a maid in the first place. They distrusted her cooking – didn't the French eat horses and frogs? But through gestures and pleading, Babette softened their hearts. She would do any chores in exchange for room and board.

For the next twelve years Babette worked for the sisters. The first time Martine showed her how to split a cod and cook the gruel, Babette's eyebrow shot upward and her nose wrinkled a little, but she never once questioned her assignments. She fed the poor people of the town and took over all house-keeping chores. She even helped with Sabbath services. Everyone had to agree that Babette brought new life to the stagnant community.

Since Babette never referred to her past life in France, it came as a great surprise to Martine and Philippa when one day, after twelve years, she received her very first letter. Babette read it, looked up to see the sisters staring at her, and announced matter-of-factly that a wonderful thing had happened to her. Each year a friend in Paris had renewed Babette's number in the French lottery. This year, her ticket had won. Ten thousand francs!

The sisters pressed Babette's hands in congratulations, but inwardly their hearts sank. They knew that soon Babette would be leaving.

As it happened, Babette's winning the lottery coincided with the very time the sisters were discussing a celebration to honor the hundredth anniversary of their father's birth. Babette came to them with a request. In twelve years I have asked nothing of you, she began. They nodded. But now I have a request: I would like to prepare the meal for the anniversary service. I would like to cook you a real French dinner.

Although the sisters had grave misgivings about this plan, Babette was certainly right that she had asked no favors in twelve years. What choice had they but to agree?

When the money arrived from France, Babette went away briefly to make arrangements for the dinner. Over the next few weeks after her return, the residents of Norre Vosburg were treated to one amazing sight after another as boats docked to unload provisions for Babette's kitchen. Workmen pushed wheelbarrows loaded with crates of small birds. Cases of champagne – *champagne!* – and wine soon followed. The entire head of a cow, fresh vegetables, truffles, pheasants, ham, strange creatures that lived in the sea, a huge tortoise still alive and moving his snakelike head from side to side – all these ended up in the sisters' kitchen now firmly ruled by Babette.

Martine and Philippa, alarmed over this apparent witch's brew, explained their predicament to the members of the sect, now old and gray and only eleven in number. Everyone clucked in sympathy. After some discussion they agreed to eat the French meal, withholding comment about it lest Babette get the wrong idea. Tongues were meant for praise and thanksgiving, not for indulging in exotic tastes.

It snowed on December 15, the day of the dinner, brightening the dull village with a gloss of white. The sisters were pleased to learn that an unexpected guest would join them: ninety-year-old Miss Loewenhielm would be escorted by her nephew, the cavalry officer who had courted Martine long ago, now a general serving in the royal palace.

Babette had somehow scrounged enough china and crystal, and had decorated the room with candles and ever-greens. Her table looked lovely. When the meal began all the villagers remembered their agreement and sat mute, like turtles around a pond. Only the general remarked on the food and drink. 'Amontillado!' he exclaimed when he raised the first glass. 'And the finest Amontillado that I have ever tasted.' When he sipped the first spoonful of soup, the general could have sworn it was turtle soup, but how could such a thing be found on the coast of Jutland?

'Incredible!' said the general when he tasted the next course. 'It is Blinis Demidoff!' All the other guests, their faces puckered with deep wrinkles, were eating the same rare delicacy without expression or comment. When the general rhapsodized about the champagne, a Veuve Cliquot 1860, Babette ordered her kitchen boy to keep the general's glass filled at all times. He alone seemed to appreciate what was set before him.

Although no one else spoke of the food or drink, gradually the banquet worked a magical effect on the churlish villagers. Their blood warmed. Their tongues loosened. They spoke of the old days when the Dean was alive and of Christmas the year the bay froze. The Brother who had cheated another on a business deal finally confessed, and the two women who had feuded found themselves conversing. A woman burped, and the Brother next to her said without thinking, 'Hallelujah!'

The general, though, could speak of nothing but the meal. When the kitchen boy brought out the *coup de grâce* (that word, again), baby quail prepared *en Sarcophage*, the general exclaimed that he had seen such a dish in only one place in Europe, the famous Café Anglais in Paris, the restaurant once renowned for its woman chef.

Heady with wine, his senses sated, unable to contain himself, the general rose to make a speech. 'Mercy and truth, my friends, have met together,' he began. 'Righteousness and bliss shall kiss one another.' And then the general had to pause, 'for he was in the habit of forming his speeches with care, conscious of his purpose, but here, in the midst of the Dean's simple congregation, it was as if the whole figure of General Loewenhielm, his breast covered with decorations, were but a mouthpiece for a message which meant to be brought forth.' The general's message was grace.

Although the Brothers and Sisters of the sect did not fully comprehend the general's speech, at that moment 'the vain illusions of this earth had dissolved before their eyes like smoke, and they had seen the universe as it really is.' The little company broke up and went outside into a town coated with glistening snow under a sky ablaze with stars.

'Babette's Feast' ends with two scenes. Outside, the old-timers join hands around the fountain and lustily sing the old songs of faith. It is a communion scene: Babette's feast opened the gate and grace stole in. They felt, adds Isak Dinesen, 'as if they had indeed had their sins washed white as wool, and in this regained innocent attire were gamboling like little lambs.'

The final scene takes place inside, in the wreck of a kitchen piled high with unwashed dishes, greasy pots, shells, carapaces, gristly bones, broken crates, vegetable trimmings, and empty bottles. Babette sits amid the mess, looking as wasted as the night she arrived twelve years before. Suddenly the sisters realize that, in accordance with the vow, no one has spoken to Babette of the dinner.

'It was quite a nice dinner, Babette,' Martine says tentatively.

Babette seems far away. After a time she says to them, 'I was once cook at the Café Anglais.'

'We will all remember this evening when you have gone back to Paris, Babette,' Martine adds, as if not hearing her.

Babette tells them that she will not be going back to Paris. All her friends and relatives there have been killed or imprisoned. And, of course, it would be expensive to return to Paris.

'But what about the ten thousand francs?' the sisters ask.

Then Babette drops the bombshell. She has spent her winnings, every last franc of the ten thousand she won, on the feast they have just devoured. Don't be shocked, she tells them. That is what a proper dinner for twelve costs at the Café Anglais.

In the general's speech, Isak Dinesen leaves no doubt that she wrote 'Babette's Feast' not simply as a story of a fine meal but as a parable of grace: a gift that costs everything for the giver and nothing for the recipient. This is what General Loewenhielm told the grim-faced parishioners gathered around him at Babette's table:

> We have all of us been told that grace is to be found in the universe. But in our human foolishness and shortsightedness we imagine divine grace to be finite. . . . But the moment comes when our eyes are opened, and we see and realize that grace is infinite. Grace, my friends, demands nothing from us but that we shall await it with confidence and acknowledge it in gratitude.

Twelve years before, Babette had landed among the graceless ones. Followers of Luther, they heard sermons on grace nearly every Sunday and the rest of the week tried to earn God's favor with their pieties and renunciations. Grace came to them in the form of a feast, Babette's feast, a meal of a life-time lavished on those who had in no way earned it, who barely possessed the faculties to receive it. Grace came to Norre Vosburg as it always comes: free of charge, no strings attached, on the house.

Who Moved the Stone

Frank Morison

This famous book addresses the momentous question: What really happened between the arrest of Jesus and the discovery of the empty tomb? It is also the inner story of a man who originally set out to write one kind of book and found himself compelled to write quite another.

ISBN: 1-85078-242-3

Price: £4.99

First published in 1930 by Faber and Faber Limited,
3 Queen Square, London WC1N 3AU
First published in Faber Paperbacks 1958
Reprinted 1959, 1962, 1963, 1965, 1967, 1969, 1971, 1972, 1975,
1978, 1981, 1983, 1987

This impression published 1983, courtesy of Faber and Faber Limited
by OM Publishing

OM Publishing is an imprint of Paternoster Publishing,
PO Box 300, Carlisle, Cumbria, CA3 0QS, UK
http://www.paternoster-publishing.com

Reprinted in 1990 (twice), 1993, 1994, 1996, 1997

1

The Book that Refused
to be Written

I suppose that most writers will confess to having hidden away somewhere in the secret recesses of their most private drawer the first rough draft of a book which, for one reason or another, will never see the light of day.

Usually it is Time – that hoary offender – who has placed his veto upon the promised task. The rough outline is drawn up in a moment of enthusiasm and exalted vision; it is worked upon for a time and then it is put aside to await that leisured 'tomorrow' which so often never comes. Other and and more pressing duties assert themselves; engagements and responsibilities multiply, and the treasured draft sinks further and deeper into its ultimate hiding-place. So the years go by, until one day the writer awakens to the knowledge that, whatever other achievements may be his, this particular book will never be written.

In the present case it was different.

It was not that the inspiration failed, or that the day of leisure never came. It was rather that when it did come the inspiration led in a new and unexpected direction. It was as though a man set out to cross a forest by a familiar and well-beaten track and came out suddenly where he did not expect to come out. The point of entry was the same; it was the point of *emergence* that was different.

Let me try to explain briefly what I mean.

When, as a very young man, I first began seriously to study the life of Christ, I did so with a very definite feeling that, if I may so put it, His history rested upon very insecure foundations.

If you will carry your mind back in imagination to the late 'nineties you will find in the prevailing intellectual attitude of that period the key to much of my thought. It is true that the absurd cult which denied even the historical existence of Jesus had ceased to carry weight. But the work of the Higher Critics – particularly the German critics – had succeeded in spreading a very prevalent impression among students that the particular form in which the narrative of His life and death had come down to us was unreliable, and that one of the four records was nothing other than a brilliant apologetic written many years, and perhaps many decades, after the first generation had passed away.

Like most other young men, deeply immersed in other things, I had no means of verifying or forming an independent judgment upon these statements, but the fact that almost every word of the Gospels was just then the subject of high wrangling and dispute did very largely colour the thought of the time, and I suppose I could hardly escape its influence.

But there was one aspect of the subject which touched me closely. I had already begun to take a deep interest in physical science, and one did not have to go very far in those days to discover that scientific thought was obstinately and even dogmatically opposed to what are called the miraculous elements in the Gospels. Very often the few things the textual critics had left standing Science proceeded to undermine. Personally I did not attach anything like the same weight to the conclusions of the textual critics that I did to this fundamental matter of the miraculous. It seemed to me that purely documentary criticism might be mistaken, but that the laws of the Universe should go back on themselves in a quite arbitrary and inconsequential manner seemed very improbable. Had not Huxley himself declared in a peculiarly final way that 'miracles do not happen', while Matthew Arnold, with his famous gospel of 'Sweet Reasonableness', had spent a great deal of his time in trying to evolve a non-miraculous Christianity?

For the person of Jesus Christ Himself, however, I had a deep and even reverent regard. He seemed to me an almost legendary figure of purity and noble manhood. A coarse word with regard to Him, or the taking of His name lightly, stung me to the quick. I am only too conscious how far this attitude fell short of the full dogmatic position of Christianity. But it is an honest statement of how at least one young student felt in those early formative years when superficial things so often obscure the deeper and more permanent realities which lie behind.

It was about this time – more for the sake of my own peace of mind than for publication – that I conceived the idea of writing a short monograph on what seemed to me to be the supremely important and critical phase in the life of Christ – the last seven days – though later I came to see that the days immediately succeeding the Crucifixion were quite as crucial. The title I chose was 'Jesus, the Last Phase', a conscious reminiscence of a famous historical study by Lord Rosebery.

I took the last seven days of the life of Jesus for three reasons:

1. This period seemed remarkably free from the miraculous element which on scientific grounds I held suspect.

2. All the Gospel writers devoted much space to this period, and, in the main, were strikingly in agreement.

3. The trial and execution of Jesus was a reverberating historical event, attested indirectly by a thousand political consequences and by a vast literature which grew out of them.

It seemed to me that if I could come at the truth *why* this man died a cruel death at the hands of the Roman Power, how He Himself regarded the matter, and especially how He behaved under the test, I should be very near to the true solution of the problem.

Such, briefly, was the purpose of the book which I had planned. I wanted to take this Last Phase of the life of Jesus, with all its quick and pulsating drama, its sharp, clear-cut background of antiquity, and its tremendous psychological and human interest – to strip it of its overgrowth of primitive beliefs and dogmatic suppositions, and to see this supremely great Person as He really was.

I need not stay to describe here how, fully ten years later, the opportunity came to study the life of Christ as I had long wanted to study it, to investigate the origins of its literature, to sift some of the evidence at first hand, and to form my own judgment on the problem which it presents. I will only say that it effected a revolution in my thought. Things emerged from that old-world story which previously I should have thought impossible. Slowly but very definitely the conviction grew that the drama of those unforgettable weeks of human history was stranger and deeper than it seemed. It was the *strangeness* of many notable things in the story which first arrested and held my interest. It was only later that the irresistible logic of their meaning came into view.

I want to try, in the remaining chapters of this book, to explain why that other venture never came to port, what were the hidden rocks upon which it foundered, and how I landed upon, to me, an unexpected shore.

2

The Real Case Against the Prisoner

In attempting to unravel the tangled skein of passions, prejudices, and political intrigues with which the last days of Jesus are interwoven, it has always seemed to me a sound principle to go straight to the heart of the mystery by studying closely the nature of the charge which was brought against Him.

I remember this aspect of the question coming home to me one morning with new and unexpected force. I tried to picture to myself what would happen if some two thousand years hence a great controversy should arise about one who was the centre of a criminal trial, say, in 1922. By that time most of the essential documents would have passed into oblivion. An old faded cutting of *The Times* or *Telegraph*, or perhaps some tattered fragment of a legal book describing the case, might have survived to reach the collection of an antiquary. From these and other fragments the necessary conclusions would have to be drawn. Is it not certain that people living in that far-off day, and desiring to get at the real truth about the man concerned, would go first to the crucial question of the charge on which he was arraigned? They would say: 'What was all the trouble about? What did his accusers say and bring against him?' If, as in the present instance, several charges appear to have been preferred, they would ask what was the *real case* against the prisoner?

Directly we set this question in the forefront of our inquiry, certain things emerge which throw new and unexpected light upon the problem. It will help us to an understanding of what these significant things are if we consider first the very singular character of the trial itself. For not only did it take place at an unprecedented hour for such proceedings, but it was marked throughout by peculiarities of a special kind. Consider in the first instance the vital element of time.

All the historians agree that the arrest of Jesus took place in the Garden of Gethsemane at a late hour on the evening immediately preceding the day of the Crucifixion, and there is strong justification for believing that it could not possibly have been earlier than eleven-thirty.

This estimate is based upon the amount of time required by the recorded events between the breaking up of the Supper Party, probably in a house in the Upper City, and the arrival of the armed band in the garden at the foot of Olivet. There are three things which point irresistibly to the hour being late:

1. The disciples were manifestly tired, and even the sturdy fisherman Peter, accustomed to lonely vigils on the deep, could not keep awake.

2. Both St. Matthew and St. Mark refer to three separate periods of slumber, broken by the periodical return of Christ from His prolonged communing under the neighbouring trees.

3. The fact that it was quite dark, and that owing to the use of torches, Christ was able to discern the approach of the arrest

party a considerable distance off (see St. Mark xiv. 42: 'Arise, let us be going: behold, he that betrayeth me is at hand.').

No one can read the records of this extraordinary episode without realizing that this particular sojourn in the garden was different from any of those previous visits to the same spot hinted at by St. John. These men were being held there by the will of Christ long after the time when they would ordinarily have been in their beds at Bethany. They were waiting at His bidding for something for which He also was waiting, and which was an unconscionably long time in coming. Assuming the supper to have been over at nine-thirty and the Garden itself reached so early as 10 p.m., the arrest could hardly have been effected much before eleven-thirty. This fixes for us with some certainty the hour of the preliminary trial.

It is generally agreed by archæologists and students of the topography of ancient Jerusalem that an old flight of steps descended from the Upper City to the gate leading to the pool of Siloam at the south-eastern angle of the City wall. It is mentioned by Nehemiah (Chap. iii. 15): 'The stairs that go down from the city of David'; and again (Chap. xii. 37): 'By the fountain gate, and straight before them, they went up by the stairs of the city of David, at the going up of the wall.'

There were thus two routes open to the arrest party. One was to follow the course of the Kedron Valley to the foot of these steps, and thence to the High Priest's house. The other was to take the main Bethany road into the new town and thence by the Tyropæan Valley to the Priestly quarter. Even if tradition had not strongly indicated the former, it is clear that to have conducted Jesus through the populous quarter of the Lower City would not only have been inexpedient, but would have necessitated a detour by which valuable time would have been lost. And in this strange nocturnal business time was a very important factor.

If, therefore, by some magic reversal of the centuries we could have stood at some vantage-point in old Jerusalem about midnight or shortly afterwards on that memorable 14 Nizan, we should probably have witnessed a small party of men leading a strangely unresisting figure through the darkness, along the rocky defile which skirted the precipitous eastern face of the Temple wall, up the historic causeway at the south-eastern angle of the City wall to the headquarters of His avowed and inveterate enemies.

How did it come about that the most distinguished Hebrew of His generation found Himself in this dangerous and menacing situation, at the dead of night, on the eve of one of the most solemn of the Jewish Festivals? What were the secret and hidden forces which precipitated His arrest? Why was this particular and highly inconvenient moment chosen? Above all, what was the gravamen of the charge which was brought against Him?

It will require very much more than this chapter to answer these questions, to which indeed the whole book is a very partial and inadequate reply. But there are two things which stand out very sharply from the records of this trial and which call for the closest study. The first is the peculiar nature of the only definite charge which was brought against Jesus. The second is the admission upon which His conviction was based.

Now it seems to me that we shall make a very grievous mistake if we assume (as has so often been done by Christian writers) that everything that the priests did that night was *ultra vires* and illegal. Of course, there are aspects of the affair which, on any reading of the case, must be considered definitely, and even flagrantly, to be at variance with the Jewish Law. That, I think, is conceded by every competent student of the Mischna and of Jewish institutions as they existed at the time.

It was illegal, for example, for the Temple Guard, acting officially as the instrument of the High Priest, to effect the arrest. That should have been left to the voluntary action of the witnesses. It was illegal to try a capital charge (Trial for Life) by night. Only 'trials for money' could be conducted after sunset. It was illegal, after the testimony of the witnesses had broken down, for the judges to cross-examine the Prisoner. They should have acquitted Him, and if the testimony given was demonstrably *false*, the witnesses should have been sentenced to death by stoning.

These things lie upon the surface of the situation. But beneath these flagrant instances of irregularity in the trial of Jesus, there runs a strong undercurrent of legality – an almost meticulous observance of certain minor points of the law – which is very illuminating and instructive to the impartial student of history.

This fact emerges very strikingly if we study the singular way in which the very ground of the accusation shifted during the course of the trial. As everyone who has atten- tively studied the records knows, there were in all three main charges brought against Jesus during the course of the successive phases of the trial. We may summarize them briefly as follows:

1. That He had threatened to destroy the Temple.
2. That He had claimed to be the Son of God.
3. That He had stirred up the people against Cæsar.

The third of these charges can be dismissed from our consideration at once. It was not the real grievance of the Jews. It was framed solely for political ends. The Roman law took no cognizance of the offences for which Christ was condemned to death, yet without Pilate the death could not be consummated. It was absolutely necessary, therefore, to find a political charge to justify before the Roman procurator the extreme penalty which they had already tacitly imposed. They chose the charge of conspiracy against Cæsar because it was the only kind of charge which would carry weight with Pontius Pilate, or indeed with any representative of the Roman Power. Even that almost failed, and would have failed completely, had the procuratorship been in stronger hands.

But, as I have said above, it does not matter what the ostensible charge before Pilate was. The thing we are concerned with very deeply is what the *real* charge of the Jews was against Christ. Directly we concentrate upon this we get an extraordinarily luminous view of what was behind the prosecution.

It must be remembered that, according to a long-established Hebrew custom, the accusers in a Jewish criminal trial were the witnesses. No other form of prosecution was legal, and the first clearly defined act in the midnight drama, after the Prisoner had been brought before the Court, was the calling of witnesses, as the law demanded. Both St. Matthew and St. Mark are quite explicit upon this point.

St. Mark says: 'Many bare false witness against him.'

St. Matthew says: 'Many false witnesses came.'

And St. Mark affirms that the evidence of these witnesses did not 'agree together' and was therefore overthrown.

To those unfamiliar with the subtleties of Jewish jurisprudence, and especially with the singular orientation of the law in favour of the prisoner, it may seem curious that, having been at considerable pains to secure witnesses for the prosecution, the Court should have proceeded forthwith to *reject* the evidence. If the story of the witnesses was a deliberate fabrication, it should not have been very difficult to have harmonized it in advance, or, in the ancient phraseology, to have made it 'agree together'. The very fact that the Court did reject the testimony proves that in this fundamental matter of the witnesses even Caiaphas himself was under some compelling necessity to follow the traditional and characteristic Hebrew usage in a 'trial for life'.

What that usage was is described for us with great wealth of detail in the Mischna. There were three classes of testimony recognized by the law:

1. A vain testimony.
2. A standing testimony.
3. An adequate testimony.

Now there was a very practical distinction between these three classes of evidence. A 'vain testimony' was testimony obviously irrelevant or worthless, and immediately recognized by the judges as such. A 'standing testimony' was evidence of a more serious kind to be accepted provisionally, until confirmed or otherwise. An 'adequate testimony' was evidence in which the witnesses 'agreed together'. 'The least discordance between the evidence of witnesses' (says the distinguished Jewish writer, Salvador) 'was held to destroy its value.'

It is clear, therefore, that whatever may have been the subject-matter of the preliminary witnesses referred to by the two Evangelists, it did not get beyond the second and provisional stage. This can only mean that it was either demonstrably contrary to the experience and knowledge of the Court, or it was invalidated on technical grounds. St. Mark's statement that it did not 'agree together' strongly indicates the latter.

But now comes a very curious thing. When this preliminary and unsatisfactory witness had been cleared away, two men came forward with a very definite and circumstantial piece of evidence.

St. Mark says:

> 'There stood up certain, and bare false witness against him, saying, We heard him say, I will destroy this temple that is made with hands, and in three days I will build another made without hands.'

St. Matthew, who in this case is probably not quoting St. Mark, but drawing upon another ancient source, confirms it by saying:

> 'But afterward came two, and said, This man said, I am able to destroy the temple of God and to build it in three days.'

Whatever else took place, therefore, on that memorable night, it seems certain that two men came forward and, with the torchlight falling full on the face of Christ, accused Him of having used words similar to these. That is a very important fact, and I will ask the reader to keep it in mind for a few moments.

Now the thing of immediate importance is to know whether these men were deliberately inventing the charge or were merely perverting for their own purpose an actual

and somewhat similar saying of Christ. Even if no other
data were available, I should personally hesitate to believe
that so definite and circumstantial a statement was a pure
invention. It is a much more deadly thing to distort what a
man has said in the hearing of others than to lie deliberately
about him. The distortion will elicit uproarious support
from overwrought and angry men. Only the most brazen
will voice approval of a deliberate and calculated lie. It
always has been so, and we can be reasonably sure that it
was so in this case. These men had heard Christ make a
resounding statement in the Temple courts, and there was
no more deadly thing which they could do than to give a
distorted and misleading version of it at His trial.

But there is another, and, to me, a very conclusive reason why we may regard the testimony of these witnesses as
a reflex of something which Christ Himself actually said
on some public occasion. Both men declared that they had
heard the Prisoner use certain words which, if substanti-
ated, involved the double offence of sorcery and sacrilege.
The penalty for sorcery was death. The penalty for sacrilege was stoning and exposure of the body. From the
standpoint of the enemies of Jesus a more fatal charge
could hardly have been laid to His account. *Yet still the
testimony was overthrown.*

Now why was that? There must be a satisfactory and
historical explanation. If the testimony of these two men
had been an absolute invention; if it had originated in the
scheming brain of Caiaphas, and the witnesses had, so to
say, been 'put up' to play their part, there would surely
have been no bungling of the affair in this naïve and exas-
perating way. After all, the witnesses had only a few words
to say, and the most elementary sort of prudence should
have secured their agreement in advance. The case against

Christ ought to have gone swiftly and triumphantly to a conviction.

But we do not find that kind of situation at all. We find a situation in which the Court, despite the illegality of its sitting at this very late hour, wasted a great deal of precious time upon a judicial process which carried it nowhere. At the end of all this elaborate hearing of witnesses Jesus Christ was virtually an unaccused, and certainly an unconvicted man. The entire proceedings threatened to break down upon a vital point of Jewish Law.

Two things emerge from this unquestionably historic fact. In the first place Caiaphas was clearly not all-powerful to work his will in that assembly. There were evidently very strong influences in the Council Chamber in favour of a rigorous observance of the law, particularly in the crucial matter of the witnesses. It must always be remembered that the judgment of this tribunal was not final. Whatever these men did that night had to pass muster the next morning before the Great Sanhedrin in plenary sitting. There had apparently been trouble once before when Nicodemus, a member of that body, had protested against condemnation without a fair hearing. They could justify the illegality of the night hearing of the case on the ground of high political necessity, and the near approach of the Feast. But any serious flaw in the accusation might easily have led to the compulsory release of the Prisoner at a moment when immense multitudes would unquestionably have flocked to His side.

The very fact, too, that the testimony was being sifted so rigorously implies a corresponding cautiousness of statement by the witnesses themselves. Under the Jewish system of jurisprudence, weighted as it undoubtedly was to lean in favour of the accused, it was a very dangerous thing to be a witness in a 'trial for life'. The penalty for uttering a false testimony was death. Hence the number of these trials was few.

But the really impressive inference from all these singular proceedings is surely this: If the testimony was *not* preconcerted; if its disagreement both surprised and exasperated the high priest, it is clear that it was at least *bona-fide* testimony, and bore some definite relation to the facts. Thus, even if the writer of St. John's Gospel had not preserved for us what we may call the 'official' version of what took place in the Temple courts, we should be compelled to believe that Jesus did upon some historical occasion use some words closely resembling those with which He was charged.

What was the historic utterance which lay behind this charge? What did Jesus really say to give rise to these circumstantial statements? There are three versions from which we may choose. According to St. Mark's 'witness' Jesus deliberately threatened to destroy the Temple and to replace it magically in three days. The words are very explicit:

'I will destroy this temple that is made with hands, and in three days I will build another made without hands.'

St. Matthew's witness modifies and softens the accusation considerably. The suggestion of the magical replacement of the Temple is still there, but Christ is represented as only claiming the *power* to do this:

'This man said, I am able to destroy the temple of God, and to build it in three days.'

Can we, in the absence of a more authentic version of what the original utterance was, accept either of these statements as the true one? Surely we cannot without doing violence to the whole Synoptic impression of the historic Jesus. For consider their import. Jesus is made to say that, of His own power and volition, He could pull down the Temple of Herod, or cause it to fall down, or disappear, and replace it by another. Such a claim could, of course, only be validated by the exercise of supernormal or magical powers beyond anything ever asserted of Christ, and beyond the wildest dreams of the most deluded disciple of Eastern necromancy. Indeed, we may say that no really sane person, especially one of the spiritual and moral category to which Christ belongs, would make a statement of this particular sort.

We can imagine some fanatical and half-witted person, whose whole mentality bordered on the insane, throwing out this preposterous boast in a sudden access of frenzy, knowing full well that he would never be called upon to justify it. But the Prisoner in this trial does not come within that definition. He does not come within a thousand miles of it. In all His story there is no trace of those characteristics which are the hall-mark of the unstable mind. On the other hand, there are many indications of that high sanity which accompanies a firmly disciplined mind. He seems to have been supremely a lover of truth and sincerity, and that inner humility which is man's greatest claim to kinship with God; He was a great hater of shams and hypocrisies and futile boasts. Moreover, He was a somewhat shy and intensely sensitive man. No one with an eye for historic truth, flashing out of the ancient pages of His record, can fail to see what happened when they brought to Him the woman taken in adultery. He *blushed*, and He stooped to write in the sand that He might cover His momentary confusion and regain the moral poise which a public situation attended with peculiarly indelicate and disgusting elements demanded. There, if anywhere, you have a glimpse of the real Jesus of history. It rings true with the memorable moral sayings recorded of Him. But it does not ring true with this grotesque and overweening boast.

The version of two witnesses, therefore, must at least be held suspect until we have corroborative testimony of the most emphatic kind. But the evidence at our disposal points in quite a different direction. According to St. John, what Jesus really did say was: 'Destroy this temple and in three days I will raise it up.' And the writer adds parenthetically: 'But he spake of the temple of his body.'

Of course, no serious student of this problem will deny for a moment that this is a difficult saying. It is difficult whatever interpretation is put upon it. But if we are to decide between three divergent and contradictory readings, I am bound to say that there is one thing which impresses me profoundly – the fact that *the words 'in three days' are found in them all*. I do not think that the immense weight of that circumstance has been fully realized.

In ordinary life, when confronted with several divergent accounts of a given happening, it is a sound and consistent rule to examine first the points upon which the narrators are agreed. The presumption that such points of agreement represent something solid and original is very strong. Particularly is this the case when the witnesses come, as it were, from opposite camps, and are in marked disagreement upon other essential features of the case.

Now the peculiarity of the phrase 'in three days' lies in the fact that it occurs very rarely in the recorded teaching of

Christ, and then only in circumstances which have seemed to many critics to present grave doubts as to the authenticity of the passages in question. Take, for example, the three outstanding instances which occur in the Gospel of St. Mark:

Mark viii. 31: 'And he began to teach them, that the Son of man must suffer many things, and be rejected by the elders, and the chief priests, and the scribes, and be killed, and after three days rise again.'

Mark ix. 31: 'For he taught his disciples, and said unto them, The Son of man is delivered up into the hands of men, and they shall kill him; and when he is killed, after three days he shall rise again.'

Mark x. 33: 'Behold, we go up to Jerusalem; and the Son of man shall be delivered unto the chief priests and the scribes; and they shall condemn him to death, and shall deliver him unto the Gentiles: and they shall mock him, and shall spit upon him, and shall scourge him, and shall kill him; and after three days he shall rise again.'

The modern reader, coming to these passages with a certain instinctive reluctance to accept anything which transcends the field of normal experience is inclined to say: 'I can understand Jesus predicting His own death. He must have foreseen what was the probable outcome of the ever-widening gap between Himself and the priests, and I think it is not unlikely that He may have prepared the disciples privately for the event. But surely these direct references to His rising from the dead can only have been written after His death and are not an integral part of the original utterances.'

Let us admit frankly that it does look like that at first sight. And yet when we come to examine closely the minutes of this trial with all its primitive marks of authenticity; its meticulous and, in the end, fruitless hearing of hostile witnesses; we make the startling discovery that these very words ('in three days') which reason asserts *could never have been uttered by Christ*, are precisely the words which according to all the witnesses formed the pith and core of the fatal and historic sentence with which He was charged. It would have been a strange coincidence indeed if the one sentence chosen by the enemies of Christ upon which to base the most deadly charge they could bring against Him found no counterpart or parallel whatever in all the varied teaching of the two preceding years.

What, then, do we find? We find the Prisoner accused of making a claim so fantastic and absurd that, even if His judges had not rejected the testimony, we should have had to receive it with the gravest possible doubt. Yet from the very texture of the circumstances there seems to emerge the fact that what He probably did say was more extraordinary still.

He said in effect: 'If you kill me, I will rise again from the grave.' I see no escape from the logic of that conclusion. We may hold that He was mistaken; that He was held by some strange mental obsession which periodically flashed out in His public utterance. But that He said this singular and almost unbelievable thing seems to me to be very nearly beyond the possibility of doubt.

The Essential John Stott

John R. W. Stott

Known worldwide as a Bible teacher, speaker and writer, John Stott can be relied upon to produce superb biblical exposition and characteristically thoughtful studies of Christian belief. *The Cross of Christ* and *The Contemporary Christian* explore his thinking on the theory and practice of Christianity.

ISBN: 0–85111–758–9

Price: £14.99

First published in 1999 by Inter-Varsity Press, England
The Book-publishing division of the
Universities and Colleges Christian Fellowship

1

The Centrality of the Cross

Do you know the painting by Holman Hunt, the leader of the Pre-Raphaelite Brotherhood, entitled 'The Shadow of Death'? It depicts the inside of the carpenter's shop in Nazareth. Stripped to the waist, Jesus stands by a wooden trestle on which he has put down his saw. He lifts his eyes towards heaven, and the look on his face is one of either pain or ecstasy or both. He also stretches, raising both arms above his head. As he does so, the evening sunlight streaming through the open door casts a dark shadow in the form of a cross on the wall behind him, where his tool-rack looks like a horizontal bar on which his hands have been crucified. The tools themselves remind us of the fateful hammer and nails.

In the left foreground a woman kneels among the wood chippings, her hands resting on the chest in which the rich gifts of the Magi are kept. We cannot see her face because she has averted it. But we know that she is Mary. She looks startled (or so it seems) at her son's cross-like shadow on the wall.

The Pre-Raphaelites have a reputation for sentimentality. Yet they were serious and sincere artists, and Holman Hunt himself was determined, as he put it, to 'do battle with the frivolous art of the day', its superficial treatment of trite themes. So he spent 1870–73 in the Holy Land, and painted 'The Shadow of Death' in Jerusalem, as he sat on the roof of his house.[1] Though the idea is historically fictitious, it is also theologically true. From Jesus' youth, indeed even from his birth, the cross cast its shadow ahead of him. His death was central to his mission. Moreover, the church has always recognized this.

Imagine a stranger visiting St Paul's Cathedral in London. Having been brought up in a non-Christian culture, he knows next to nothing about Christianity. Yet he is more than a tourist; he is personally interested and keen to learn.

Walking along Fleet Street, he is impressed by the grandeur of the building's proportions, and marvels that Sir Christopher Wren could have conceived such an edifice after the Great Fire of London in 1666. As his eyes attempt to take it in, he cannot help noticing the huge golden cross which dominates the dome.

He enters the cathedral and stands at its central point, under the dome. Trying to grasp the size and shape of the building, he becomes aware that its ground plan, consisting of nave and transepts, is cruciform. He walks round and observes that each side chapel contains what looks to him like a table, on which, prominently displayed, there stands a cross. He goes downstairs into the crypt to see the tombs of famous men such as Sir Christopher Wren himself, Lord Nelson and the Duke of Wellington: a cross is engraved or embossed on each.

---

[1] See *Pre-Raphaelite Paintings* from the Manchester City Art Gallery, where 'The Shadow of Death' hangs, by Julian Treuherz.

Returning upstairs, he decides to remain for the service which is about to begin. The man beside him is wearing a little cross on his lapel, while the lady on his other side has one on her necklace. His eye now rests on the colourful, stained-glass east window. Though he cannot make out the details from where he is sitting, he cannot fail to notice that it contains a cross.

Suddenly, the congregation stands up. The choir and clergy enter, preceded by somebody carrying a processional cross. They are singing a hymn. The visitor looks down at the service paper to read its opening words:

> We sing the praise of him who died,
>   Of him who died upon the cross;
> The sinner's hope let men deride,
>   For this we count the world but loss.

From what follows he comes to realize that he is witnessing a Holy Communion service, and that this focuses upon the death of Jesus. For when the people around him go forward to the communion rail to receive bread and wine, the minister speaks to them of the body and blood of Christ. The service ends with another hymn:

> When I survey the wondrous cross
>   On which the Prince of glory died,
> My richest gain I count but loss,
>   And pour contempt on all my pride.
>
> Forbid it, Lord, that I should boast
>   Save in the cross of Christ my God;
> All the vain things that charm me most,
>   I sacrifice them to his blood.

Although the congregation now disperses, a family stays behind. They have brought their child to be baptized. Joining them at the font, the visitor sees the minister first pour water over the child and then trace a cross on its forehead, saying 'I sign you with the cross, to show that you must not be ashamed to confess the faith of Christ crucified . . .'.

The stranger leaves the cathedral impressed, but puzzled. The repeated insistence by word and symbol on the centrality of the cross has been striking. Yet questions have arisen in his mind. Some of the language used has seemed exaggerated. Do Christians really for the sake of the cross 'count the world but loss', and 'boast' in it alone, and 'sacrifice' everything for it? Can the Christian faith be accurately summed up as 'the faith of Christ crucified'? What are the grounds, he asks himself, for this concentration on the cross of Christ?

The sign and symbol of the cross

Every religion and ideology has its visual symbol, which illustrates a significant feature of its history or beliefs. The lotus flower, for example, although it was used by the ancient Chinese, Egyptians and Indians, is now particularly associated with Buddhism. Because of its wheel shape it is thought to depict either the cycle of birth and death or the emergence of beauty and harmony out of the muddy waters of chaos. Sometimes the Buddha is portrayed as enthroned in a fully open lotus flower.

Ancient Judaism avoided visual signs and symbols, for fear of infringing the second commandment which prohibits the manufacture of images. But modern Judaism now employs the so-called Shield or Star of David, a hexagram formed by combining two equilateral triangles. It speaks of God's covenant with David that his throne would be established for ever and that the Messiah would be descended from him. Islam, the other monotheistic faith which arose in the Middle East, is symbolized by a crescent, at least in West Asia. Originally depicting a phase of the moon, it was already the symbol of sovereignty in Byzantium before the Muslim conquest.

The secular ideologies of this century also have their universally recognizable signs. The Marxist hammer and sickle, adopted in 1917 by the Soviet government from a nineteenth-century Belgian painting, represent industry and agriculture; and they are crossed to signify the union of workers and peasants, of factory and field. The swastika, on the other hand, has been traced back some 6,000 years. The arms of its cross are bent clockwise to symbolize either the movement of the sun across the sky, or the cycle of the four seasons, or the process of creativity and prosperity ('svasti' being a Sanskrit word for 'well-being'). At the beginning of this century, however, it was taken up by some German groups as a symbol of the Aryan race. Then Hitler took it over, and it became the sinister sign of Nazi racial bigotry.

Christianity, then, is no exception in having a visual symbol. The cross was not its earliest, however. Because of the wild accusations which were levelled against Christians, and the persecution to which they were exposed, they 'had to be very circumspect and to avoid flaunting their religion. Thus the cross, now the universal symbol of Christianity, was at first avoided, not only for its direct association with Christ, but for its shameful association with the execution of a common criminal also'.[2] So on the walls and ceilings of the catacombs (underground burial-places outside Rome, where the persecuted Christians probably hid), the earliest Christian motifs seem to have been either non-committal paintings of a peacock (supposed to symbolize immortality), a dove, the athlete's victory palm or, in particular, a fish. Only the initiated would know, and nobody else could guess, that *ichthys* ('fish') was an acronym for *Iesus Christos Theou Huios Soter* ('Jesus Christ, Son of God, Saviour'). But it did not remain the Christian sign, doubtless because the association between Jesus and a fish was purely acronymic (a fortuitous arrangement of letters) and had no visual significance.

Somewhat later, probably during the second century, the persecuted Christians seem to have preferred to paint biblical themes like Noah's ark, Abraham killing the ram instead of Isaac, Daniel in the lions' den, his three friends in the fiery furnace, Jonah being disgorged by the fish, some baptisms, a shepherd carrying a lamb, the healing of the paralytic and the raising of Lazarus. All these were symbolic of Christ's redemption, while not being in themselves incriminating, since only the instructed would have been able to interpret their meaning. In addition, the Chi-Rho monogram (the first two letters of the Greek word *Christos*) was a popular cryptogram, often in the form of a cross, and sometimes with a lamb standing before it, or with a dove.

A universally acceptable Christian emblem would obviously need to speak of Jesus Christ, but there was a wide range of possibilities. Christians might have chosen

---

[2] Michael Gough, *Origins of Christian Art*, p. 18. See also J. H. Miller, 'Cross' and 'Crucifix'; *Christian World*, ed. Geoffrey Barraclough; and *Cross and Crucifix* by Cyril E. Pocknee.

the crib or manager in which the baby Jesus was laid, or the carpenter's bench at which he worked as a young man in Nazareth, dignifying manual labour, or the boat from which he taught the crowds in Galilee, or the apron he wore when washing the apostles' feet, which would have spoken of his spirit of humble service. Then there was the stone which, having been rolled from the mouth of Joseph's tomb, would have proclaimed his resurrection. Other possibilities were the throne, symbol of divine sovereignty, which John in his vision of heaven saw that Jesus was sharing, or the dove, symbol of the Holy Spirit sent from heaven on the Day of Pentecost. Any of these seven symbols would have been suitable as a pointer to some aspect of the ministry of the Lord. But instead the chosen symbol came to be a simple cross. Its two bars were already a cosmic symbol from remote antiquity of the axis between heaven and earth. But its choice by Christians had a more specific explanation. They wished to commemorate as central to their understanding of Jesus neither his birth nor his youth, neither his teaching nor his service, neither his resurrection nor his reign, nor his gift of the Spirit, but his death, his crucifixion. The crucifix (that is, a cross to which a figure of Christ is attached) does not appear to have been used before the sixth century.

It seems certain that, at least from the second century onwards, Christians not only drew, painted and engraved the cross as a pictorial symbol of their faith, but also made the sign of the cross on themselves or others. One of the first witnesses to this practice was Tertullian, the North African lawyer-theologian who flourished about AD 200. He wrote:

At every forward step and movement, at every going in and out, when we put on our clothes and shoes, when we bathe, when we sit at table, when we light the lamps, on couch, on seat, in all the ordinary actions of daily life, we trace upon the forehead the sign [the cross].[3]

Hippolytus, the scholar-presbyter of Rome, is a particularly interesting witness, because he is known to have been 'an avowed reactionary who in his own generation stood for the past rather than the future'. His famous treatise *The Apostolic Tradition* (*c.* AD 215) 'claims explicitly to be recording only the forms and models of rites *already* traditional and customs *already* long-established, and to be written in deliberate protest against innovations'.[4] When he describes certain 'church observances', therefore, we may be sure that they were already being practised a generation or more previously. He mentions that the sign of the cross was used by the bishop when anointing the candidate's forehead at Confirmation, and he recommends it in private prayer: 'imitate him (Christ) always, by signing thy forehead sincerely: for this is the sign of his passion.' It is also, he adds, a protection against evil: 'When tempted, always reverently seal thy forehead with the sign of the cross. For this sign of the passion is displayed and made manifest against the devil if thou makest it in faith, not in order that thou mayest be seen of men, but by thy knowledge putting it forth as a shield.'[5]

There is no need for us to dismiss this habit as superstitious. In origin at least, the sign of the cross was intended to identify and indeed sanctify each act as belonging to Christ.

---

[3] Tertullian, *De Corona*, Ch. III, p. 94.

[4] Gregory Dix (ed.), *Apostolic Tradition of St Hippolytus*, p. xi.

[5] *Ibid.*, pp. 68–69.

In the middle of the third century, when another North African, Cyprian, was Bishop of Carthage, a terrible persecution was unleashed by the Emperor Decius (AD 250–251) during which thousands of Christians died rather than offer sacrifice to his name. Anxious to strengthen the morale of his people, and to encourage them to accept martyrdom rather than compromise their Christian faith, Cyprian reminded them of the ceremony of the cross: 'let us take also for protection of our head the helmet of salvation . . . that our brow may be fortified, so as to keep safe the sign of God.'[6] As for the faithful who endured prison and risked death, Cyprian praised them in these terms: 'your brows, hallowed by God's seal . . . reserved themselves for the crown which the Lord would give.'[7]

Richard Hooker, the sixteenth-century Anglican theologian and Master of the Temple in London, applauded the fact that the early church Fathers, in spite of heathen scorn at the sufferings of Christ, 'chose rather the sign of the cross (*sc.* in baptism) than any other outward mark, whereby the world might most easily discern always what they were.'[8] He was aware of the forthright objections of the Puritans. 'Crossing and such like pieces of Popery,' they were saying, 'which the church of God in the Apostles' time never knew', ought not to be used, for human inventions ought not to be added to divine institutions, and there was always the danger of superstitious misuse. As King Hezekiah destroyed the brazen serpent, so crossing should be abandoned. But Hooker stood his ground. In

---

[6] Cyprian, *Ad Thibaritanos* IX.

[7] Cyprian, *De Lapsis* 2.

[8] Richard Hooker, *Ecclesiastical Polity*, Book V, Ch. lxv. 20, 'Of the Cross in Baptism'.

'matters indifferent', which were not incompatible with Scripture, Christians were free. Besides, the sign of the cross had a positive usefulness: it is 'for us an admonition . . . to glory in the service of Jesus Christ, and not to hang down our heads as men ashamed thereof, although it procure us reproach and obloquy at the hands of this wretched world'.[9]

It was Constantine, the first emperor to profess to be a Christian, who gave added impetus to the use of the cross symbol. For (according to Eusebius), on the eve of the Battle of Milvian Bridge which brought him supremacy in the West (AD 312–313), he saw a cross of light in the sky, along with the words *in hoc signo vinces* ('conquer by this sign'). He immediately adopted it as his emblem, and had it emblazoned on the standards of his army.

Whatever we may think of Constantine and of the development of post-Constantinian 'Christendom', at least the church has faithfully preserved the cross as its central symbol. In some ecclesiastical traditions the candidate for baptism is still marked with this sign, and the relatives of a Christian who after death is buried rather than cremated are likely to have a cross erected over his grave. Thus from Christian birth to Christian death, as we might put it, the church seeks to identify and protect us with a cross.

The Christians' choice of a cross as the symbol of their faith is the more surprising when we remember the horror with which crucifixion was regarded in the ancient world. We can understand why Paul's 'message of the cross' was to many of his listeners 'foolishness', even 'madness' (1 Cor. 1:18, 23). How could any sane person worship as a god a dead man who had been justly condemned as a criminal and

---

[9] *Ibid.*, Book V. Ch. lxv. 6.

subjected to the most humiliating form of execution? This combination of death, crime and shame put him beyond the pale of respect, let alone of worship.[10]

Crucifixion seems to have been invented by 'barbarians' on the edge of the known world, and taken over from them by both Greeks and Romans. It is probably the most cruel method of execution ever practised, for it deliberately delayed death until maximum torture had been inflicted. The victim could suffer for days before dying. When the Romans adopted it, they reserved it for criminals convicted of murder, rebellion or armed robbery, provided that they were also slaves, foreigners or other non-persons. The Jews were therefore outraged when the Roman general Varus crucified 2,000 of their compatriots in 4 BC, and when during the siege of Jerusalem the general Titus crucified so many fugitives from the city that neither 'space . . . for the crosses, for crosses for the bodies' could be found.[11]

Roman citizens were exempt from crucifixion, except in extreme cases of treason. Cicero in one of his speeches condemned it as *crudelissimum taeterrimumque supplicium*, 'a most cruel and disgusting punishment'.[12] A little later he declared: 'To bind a Roman citizen is a crime, to flog him is an abomination, to kill him is almost an act of murder: to crucify him is – What? There is no fitting word that can possibly describe so horrible a deed.'[13] Cicero was even

---

[10] See especially pp. 1–10 of *Crucifixion* by Martin Hengel, whose original title was *Mors turpissima crucis*, 'the utterly vile death of the cross', an expression first used by Origen.

[11] See the accounts given by Josephus in *Antiquities* xvii. 10.10 and *Jewish War* V.xi.1.

[12] Cicero, *Against Verres* II. v. 64, para. 165.

[13] *Ibid.*, II. v. 66, para. 170.

more explicit in his successful defence in 63 BC of the elderly senator Gaius Rabirius who had been charged with murder: 'the very word "cross" should be far removed not only from the person of a Roman citizen, but from his thoughts, his eyes and his ears. For it is not only the actual occurrence of these things (sc. the procedures of crucifixion) or the endurance of them, but liability to them, the expectation, indeed the mere mention of them, that is unworthy of a Roman citizen and a free man.'[14]

If the Romans regarded crucifixion with horror, so did the Jews, though for a different reason. They made no distinction between 'tree' and a 'cross', and so between a hanging and a crucifixion. They therefore automatically applied to crucified criminals the terrible statement of the law that 'anyone who is hung on a tree under God's curse' (Dt. 21:23). They could not bring themselves to believe that God's Messiah would die under his curse, strung up on a tree. As Trypho the Jew put it to Justin the Christian apologist, who engaged him in dialogue: 'I am exceedingly incredulous on this point.'[15]

So then, whether their background was Roman or Jewish or both, the early enemies of Christianity lost no opportunity to ridicule the claim that God's anointed and man's Saviour ended His life on a cross. The idea was crazy. This is well illustrated by a graffito from the second century, discovered on the Palatine Hill in Rome, on the wall of a house considered by some scholars to have been used as a school for imperial pages. It is the first surviving picture of the crucifixion, and is a caricature. A crude drawing depicts, stretched on a cross, a man with the head of a donkey. To the

---

[14] Cicero, *In Defence of Rabirius* V. 16, p. 467.

[15] Justin Martyr, *Dialogue with Trypho a Jew*, Ch. lxxxix.

left stands another man, with one arm raised in worship. Unevenly scribbled underneath are the words ALEXAMENOS CEBETE (*sc. sebete*) THEON, 'Alexamenos worships God'. The cartoon is now in the Kircherian Museum in Rome. Whatever the origin of the accusation of donkey-worship (which was attributed to both Jews and Christians), it was the concept of worshipping a crucified man which was being held up to derision.

One detects the same note of scorn in Lucian of Samosata, the second-century pagan satirist. In *The Passing of Peregrinus* (a fictitious Christian convert whom he portrays as a charlatan) he lampoons Christians as 'worshipping that crucified sophist himself and living under his laws' (p. 15).

The perspective of Jesus

The fact that a cross became the Christian symbol, and that Christians stubbornly refused, in spite of the ridicule, to discard it in favour of something less offensive, can have only one explanation. It means that the centrality of the cross originated in the mind of Jesus himself. It was out of loyalty to him that his followers clung so doggedly to this sign. What evidence is there, then, that the cross stood at the centre of Jesus' own perspective?

Our only glimpse into the developing mind of the boy Jesus has been given us in the story of how at the age of 12 he was taken to Jerusalem at Passover and then left behind by mistake. When his parents found him in the temple, 'sitting among the teachers, listening to them and asking them questions', they scolded him. They had been anxiously searching for him, they said. 'Why were you searching for

me?' he responded with innocent astonishment. 'Didn't
you know I had to be in my Father's house?' (Lk. 2:41–50).
Luke tells the story with a tantalizing economy of detail.
We must therefore be careful not to read into it more than
the narrative itself warrants. This much we may affirm,
however, that already at the age of 12 Jesus was both speaking of God as 'my Father' and also feeling an inward
compulsion to occupy himself with his Father's affairs. He
knew he had a mission. His Father had sent him into the
world for a purpose. This mission he must perform; this
purpose he must fulfil. What these were emerges gradually
in the narrative of the Gospels.

The evangelists hint that Jesus' baptism and temptation
were both occasions on which he committed himself to go
God's way rather than the devil's, the way of suffering and
death rather than of popularity and acclaim. Yet Mark
(who is followed in this by Matthew and Luke) pinpoints a
later event when Jesus began to teach this clearly. It was the
watershed in his public ministry. Having withdrawn with
his apostles to the northern district round Caesarea Philippi
in the foothills of Mount Hermon, he put to them the
direct question who they thought he was. When Peter
blurted out that he was God's Messiah, immediately Jesus
'warned them not to tell anyone about him' (Mk. 8:
29–30). This injunction was consistent with his previous
instructions about keeping the so-called 'Messianic secret'.
Yet now something new took place: Jesus

> then began to teach them that the Son of Man must suffer
> many things and be rejected by the elders, chief priests and
> teachers of the law, and that he must be killed and after three
> days rise again. He spoke plainly about this (Mk. 8:31–32).

'Plainly' translates *parresia*, meaning 'with freedom of speech' or 'openly'. There was to be no secret about this. The fact of his Messiahship had been secret, because its character had been misunderstood. The popular Messianic expectation was of a revolutionary political leader. John tells us that at the peak of Jesus' Galilean popularity, after feeding the five thousand, the crowds had 'intended to come and make him king by force' (Jn. 6:15). Now that the apostles had clearly recognized and confessed his identity, however, he could explain the nature of his Messiahship and do so openly. Peter rebuked him, horrified by the fate he had predicted for himself. But Jesus rebuked Peter in strong language. The same apostle who in confessing Jesus' divine Messiahship had received a revelation from the Father (Mt. 16:17), had been deceived by the devil to deny the necessity of the cross. 'Out of my sight, Satan!' Jesus said, with a vehemence which must have astonished his hearers. 'You do not have in mind the things of God, but the things of men.'[16]

This incident is usually referred to as the first 'prediction of the passion'. There had been passing allusions before (*e.g.* Mk. 2:19–20); but this was quite unambiguous. The second was made a little later, as Jesus was passing through Galilee incognito. He said to the Twelve:

> 'The Son of Man is going to be betrayed into the hands of men. They will kill him, and after three days he will rise' (Mk. 9:31).

Mark says that the disciples did not understand what he meant, and were afraid to ask him. Matthew adds that they were 'filled with grief' (Mk. 9:30–32; *cf.* Mt. 17:22–23).

---

[16] Mk. 8:31ff.; *cf.* Mt. 16:21ff.; Lk. 9:22ff.

This was probably the time when, according to Luke, Jesus 'resolutely set out for Jerusalem' (9:51). He was determined to fulfil what had been written of him.

Jesus made his third 'prediction of the passion' when they were heading for the Holy City. Mark introduces it with a graphic description of the awe which the Lord's resolution inspired in them:

> They were on their way up to Jerusalem, with Jesus leading the way, and the disciples were astonished, while those who followed were afraid. Again he took the Twelve aside and told them what was going to happen to him. 'We are going up to Jerusalem,' he said, 'and the Son of Man will be betrayed to the chief priests and teachers of the law. They will condemn him to death and will hand him over to the Gentiles, who will mock him and spit on him, flog him and kill him. Three days later he will rise.'

Luke adds his comment that 'everything that is written by the prophets about the Son of Man will be fulfilled'.[17]

This threefold repetition of the passion prediction adds a note of solemnity to Mark's narrative. It is in this way that he deliberately prepares his readers, as Jesus deliberately prepared the Twelve, for the terrible events which were to take place. Putting the three predictions together, the most impressive emphasis is neither that Jesus would be betrayed, rejected and condemned by his own people and their leaders, nor that they would hand him over to the Gentiles who would first mock and then kill him, nor that after three days he would rise from death. It is not even that each time Jesus designates himself 'Son of Man' (the heavenly figure whom

---

[17] Mk. 10:32–34; *cf.* Mt. 20:17–19; Lk. 18:31–34.

Daniel saw in his vision, coming in the clouds of heaven, being given authority, glory and sovereign power, and receiving the worship of the nations) and yet paradoxically states that as Son of Man he will suffer and die, thus with daring originality combining the two Old Testament Messianic figures, the Suffering Servant of Isaiah 53 and the reigning Son of Man of Daniel 7. More impressive still is the determination he both expressed and exemplified. He *must* suffer and be rejected and die, he said. Everything written of him in Scripture *must* be fulfilled. So he set his face towards Jerusalem, and went ahead of the Twelve in the road. Peter's negative comment he instantly recognized as Satanic and therefore instantly repudiated.

Although these three predictions form an obvious trio because of their similar structure and wording, the Gospels record at least eight more occasions on which Jesus alluded to his death. Coming down from the mountain where he had been transfigured, he warned that he would suffer at the hands of his enemies just as John the Baptist had done,[18] and in response to the outrageously selfish request of James and John for the best seats in the kingdom, he said that he himself had come to serve, not to be served, and 'to give his life as a ransom for many'.[19] The remaining six allusions were all made during the last week of his life, as the crisis drew near. He saw his death as the culmination of centuries of Jewish rejection of God's message, and foretold that God's judgment would bring Jewish national privilege to an end.[20] Then on the Tuesday, mentioning the Passover, he said he was going to be 'handed over to be crucified'; in

---

[18] Mt. 17:9–13; Mk. 9:9–13; *cf.* Lk. 9:44.

[19] Mk. 10:35–45; Mt. 20:20–28.

[20] Mk. 12:1–12; *cf.* Mt. 21:33–46; Lk. 20:9–19.

the Bethany home he described the pouring of perfume over his head as preparing him for burial; in the upper room he insisted that the Son of Man would go just as it was written about him, and gave them bread and wine as emblems of his body and blood, thus foreshadowing his death and requesting its commemoration. Finally, in the Garden of Gethsemane he refused to be defended by men or angels, since 'how then would the Scriptures be fulfilled that say it must happen in this way?'[21] Thus the Synoptic evangelists bear a common witness to the fact that Jesus both clearly foresaw and repeatedly foretold his coming death.

John omits these precise predictions. Yet he bears witness to the same phenomenon by his seven references to Jesus' 'hour' (usually *hōra* but once *kairos*, 'time'). It was the hour of his destiny, when he would leave the world and return to the Father. Moreover, his hour was in the Father's control, so that at first it was 'not yet', though in the end he could confidently say 'the hour has come'.

When Jesus said to his mother at the Cana wedding after the wine had run out, and to his brothers when they wanted him to go to Jerusalem and advertise himself publicly, 'My time has not yet come', the surface meaning was plain. But John intended his readers to detect the deeper meaning, even though Jesus' mother and brothers did not.[22] John continues to share this secret with his readers,

---

[21] For the Passover saying see Mt. 26:2; for the 'burial' references Mk. 14:3–9 and *cf.* Mt. 26:6–13; for the woe on Judas Mk. 14:10 ff. and *cf.* Mt. 26:14 ff. and Lk. 22:22; for the institution of the supper Mk. 14:22–25 and *cf.* Mt. 26:26–29, Lk. 22:14–20 and 1 Cor. 11:23–26; and for the arrest Mt. 26:47–56 and *cf.* Mk. 14:43–50, Lk. 22:47–53 and Jn. 18:1–11.

[22] Jn. 2:4; 7:8.

and uses it to explain why Jesus' apparently blasphemous statements did not lead to his arrest. 'They tried to seize him,' he comments, 'but no-one laid a hand on him, because his time had not yet come.'[23] Only when Jesus reaches Jerusalem for the last time does John make the reference explicit. When some Greeks asked to see him, he first said, 'The hour has come for the Son of Man to be glorified' and then, after speaking plainly of his death, he went on: 'Now my heart is troubled, and what shall I say? "Father, save me from this hour"? No, it was for this very reason I came to this hour. Father, glorify your name!'[24] Then twice in the upper room he made final references to the time having come for him to leave the world and to be glorified.[25]

However uncertain we may feel about the earlier allusions to his 'hour' or 'time', we can be in no doubt about the last three. For Jesus specifically called his 'hour' the time of his 'glorification', which (as we shall see later) began with his death, and added that he could not ask to be delivered from it because this was the reason he had come into the world. Indeed, the paradox John records can hardly have been accidental, that the hour for which he had come into the world was the hour in which he left it. Mark makes matters yet more explicit by identifying his 'hour' with his 'cup'.[26]

From this evidence supplied by the Gospel writers, what are we justified in saying about Jesus' perspective on his own death? Beyond question he knew that it was going to

---

[23] Jn. 7:25 ff. especially v.30, and 8:12 ff. especially v.20.

[24] Jn. 12:20–28.

[25] Jn. 13:1; 17:1.

[26] Jn. 12:27; 13:1; Mk. 14:35, 41. *Cf.* Mt. 26:18.

happen – not in the sense that all of us know we will have to die one day, but in the sense that he would meet a violent, premature, yet purposive death. More than that, he gives three intertwining reasons for its inevitability.

First, he knew he would die because of the hostility of the Jewish national leaders. It appears that this was aroused quite early during the public ministry. His attitude to the law in general, and to the sabbath in particular, incensed them. When he insisted on healing a man with a shrivelled hand in a synagogue on a sabbath day, Mark tells us that 'the Pharisees went out and began to plot with the Herodians how they might kill Jesus' (3:6). Jesus must have been aware of this. He was also very familiar with the Old Testament record of the persecution of the faithful prophets.[27] Although he knew himself to be more than a prophet, he also knew he was not less, and that therefore he could expect similar treatment. He was a threat to the leaders' position and prejudices. According to Luke, after his reading and exposition of Isaiah 61 in the Nazareth synagogue, in which he seemed to be teaching a divine preference for the Gentiles, 'all the people in the synagogue were furious. . . . They got up, drove him out of the town, and took him to the brow of the hill on which the town was built, in order to throw him down the cliff'. Luke adds that 'he walked right through the crowd and went on his way' (4:16–30). But it was a narrow escape. Jesus knew that sooner or later they would get him.

Secondly, he knew he would die because that is what stood written of the Messiah in the Scriptures. 'The Son of Man will go just as it is written about him' (Mk. 14:21).

---

[27] Joachim Jeremias develops this argument in *Central Message*. See especially p. 41.

Indeed, when referring to the Old Testament prophetic witness, he tended to couple the death and resurrection, the sufferings and glory, of the Messiah. For the Scriptures taught both. And the Lord was still insisting on this after he had risen. He said to the disciples on the road to Emmaus: ' "Did not the Christ have to suffer these things and then enter his glory?" And beginning with Moses and all the Prophets, he explained to them what was said in all the Scriptures concerning himself' (Lk. 24:25–27; *cf.* verses 44–47).

One would dearly love to have been present at this exposition of 'Christ in all the Scriptures'. For the actual number of his recognizable quotations from the Old Testament, in relation to the cross and resurrection, is not large. He predicted the falling away of the apostles by quoting from Zechariah that when the shepherd was struck the sheep would be scattered.[28] He concluded his Parable of the Tenants with a telling reference to the stone which, though rejected by the builders, subsequently became the building's capstone or cornerstone.[29] And while hanging on the cross, three of his so-called 'seven words' were direct quotations from Scripture: 'My God, my God, why have you forsaken me?' being Psalm 22:1, 'I thirst' coming from Psalm 69:21, and 'Father, into your hands I commit my spirit' from Psalm 31:5. These three psalms all describe the deep anguish of an innocent victim, who is suffering both physically and mentally at the hands of his enemies, but who at the same time maintains his trust in his God. Although of course they were written to express the distress

---

[28] Zc. 13:7; Mt. 26:31; Mk. 14:27.

[29] Ps. 118:22; Mt. 21:42; Mk. 12:10–11; Lk. 20:17. *Cf.* Acts 4:11; 1 Pet. 2:7.

of the psalmist himself, yet Jesus had evidently come to see himself and his own sufferings as their ultimate fulfilment.

It is, however, from Isaiah 53 that Jesus seems to have derived the clearest forecast not only of his sufferings, but also of his subsequent glory. For there the servant of Yahweh is first presented as 'despised and rejected by men, a man of sorrows, and familiar with suffering' (v. 3), on whom the Lord laid our sins, so that 'he was pierced for our transgressions' and 'crushed for our iniquities' (vv. 5–6), and then, at the end of both chapters 52 and 53, is 'raised and lifted up and highly exalted' (52:13) and receives 'a portion among the great' (53:12), as a result of which he will 'sprinkle many nations' (52:15) and 'justify many' (53:11). The only straight quotation which is recorded from Jesus' lips is from verse 12, 'he was numbered with the transgressors'. 'I tell you that this must be fulfilled in me,' he said (Lk. 22:37). Nevertheless, when he declared that he 'must suffer many things' and had 'not come to be served, but to serve, and to give his life as a ransom for many' (Mk. 8:31; 10:45), although these are not direct quotations from Isaiah 53, yet their combination of suffering, service and death for the salvation of others points straight in that direction. Moreover Paul, Peter, Matthew, Luke and John – the major contributors to the New Testament – together allude to at least eight of the chapter's twelve verses. What was the origin of their confident, detailed application of Isaiah 53 to Jesus? They must have derived it from his own lips. It was from this chapter more than from any other that he learnt that the vocation of the Messiah was to suffer and die for human sin, and so be glorified.

The opposition of the hierarchy and the predictions of Scripture, however, do not in themselves explain the inevitability of Jesus' death. The third and most important reason why he knew he would die was because of his own deliberate choice. He was determined to fulfil what was written of the Messiah, however painful it would be. This was neither fatalism nor a martyr complex. It was quite simply that he believed Old Testament Scripture to be his Father's revelation and that he was totally resolved to do his Father's will and finish his Father's work. Besides, his suffering and death would not be purposeless. He had come 'to seek and to save what was lost' (Lk. 19:10). It was for the salvation of sinners that he would die, giving his life as a ransom to set them free (Mk. 10:45). So he set his face steadfastly to go to Jerusalem. Nothing would deter or deflect him. Hence the reiterated 'must' when he spoke of his death. The Son of Man *must* suffer many things and be rejected. Everything that was written about him *must* be fulfilled. He refused to appeal for angels to rescue him, because then the Scriptures would not be fulfilled which said that it *must* happen in this way. Was it not *necessary* for the Christ to suffer before entering his glory?[30] He felt under constraint, even under compulsion: 'I have a baptism to undergo, and how distressed I am (RSV "constrained", literally 'hemmed in') until it is completed!' (Lk. 12:50).

So then, although he knew he must die, it was not because he was the helpless victim either of evil forces arrayed against him, or of any inflexible fate decreed for him, but because he freely embraced the purpose of his Father for the salvation of sinners, as it had been revealed in Scripture.

This was the perspective of Jesus on his death. Despite the great importance of his teaching, his example, and his

---

[30] Mk. 8:31; Lk. 24:44; Mt. 26:54; Lk. 24:26.

works of compassion and power, none of these was central to his mission. What dominated his mind was not the living but the giving of his life. This final self-sacrifice was his 'hour', for which he had come into the world. And the four evangelists, who bear witness to him in the Gospels, show that they understand this by the disproportionate amount of space which they give to the story of his last few days on earth, his death and resurrection. It occupies between a third and a quarter of the three Synoptic Gospels, while John's Gospel has justly been described as having two parts, 'the Book of the Signs' and 'the Book of the Passion', since John spends an almost equal amount of time on each.

Left Behind

Tim La Haye & Jerry B. Jenkins

In one cataclysmic moment, millions around the globe disappear. In the midst of the chaos, pilot Rayford Steele must search for his family, for answers and for truth. As devastating as the disappearances have been, the darkest days may lie ahead. Guaranteed to tingle your spine and challenge your mind.

ISBN: 0-8423-2912-9

Price: £7.99

1

Rayford Steele's mind was on a woman he had never touched. With his fully loaded 747 on autopilot above the Atlantic en route to a 6 A.M. landing at Heathrow, Rayford had pushed from his mind thoughts of his family.

Over spring break he would spend time with his wife and twelve-year-old-son. Their daughter would be home from college, too. But for now, with his first officer dozing, Rayford imagined Hattie Durham's smile and looked forward to their next meeting.

Hattie was Rayford's senior flight attendant. He hadn't seen her in more than an hour.

Rayford used to look forward to getting home to his wife. Irene was attractive and vivacious enough, even at forty. But lately he had found himself repelled by her obsession with religion. It was all she could talk about.

God was OK with Rayford Steele. Rayford even enjoyed church occasionally. But since Irene had hooked up with a smaller congregation and was into weekly Bible studies and church every Sunday, Rayford had become uncomfortable. Hers was not a church where people gave you the benefit of the doubt, assumed the best about you, and let you be. People there had actually asked him, to his face, what God was doing in his life.

'Blessing my socks off' had become the smiling response that seemed to satisfy them, but he found more and more excuses to be busy on Sundays.

Rayford tried to tell himself it was his wife's devotion to a divine suitor that caused his mind to wander. But he knew the real reason was his own libido.

Besides, Hattie Durham was drop-dead gorgeous. No one could argue that. What he enjoyed most was that she was a toucher. Nothing inappropriate, nothing showy. She simply touched his arm as she brushed past or rested her hand gently on his shoulder when she stood behind his seat in the cockpit.

It wasn't her touch alone that made Rayford enjoy her company. He could tell from her expressions, her demeanor, her eye contact that she at least admired and respected him. Whether she was interested in anything more, he could only guess. And so he did.

They had spent time together, chatting for hours over drinks or dinner, sometimes with coworkers, sometimes not. He had not returned so much as one brush of a finger, but his eyes had held her gaze, and he could only assume his smile had made its point.

Maybe today. Maybe this morning, if her coded tap on the door didn't rouse his first officer, he would reach and cover the hand on his shoulder – in a friendly way he hoped she would recognize as a step, a first from his side, toward a relationship.

And a first it would be. He was no prude, but Rayford had never been unfaithful to Irene. He'd had plenty of opportunities. He had long felt guilty about a private necking session he enjoyed at a company Christmas party more than twelve years before. Irene had stayed home, uncomfortably past her ninth month carrying their surprise tagalong son, Ray Jr.

Though under the influence, Rayford had known enough to leave the party early. It was clear Irene noticed he was slightly drunk, but she couldn't have suspected anything else, not from her straight-arrow captain. He was the pilot who had once consumed two martinis during a snowy shutdown at O'Hare and then voluntarily grounded himself when the weather cleared. He offered to pay for bringing in a relief pilot, but Pan-Continental was so impressed that instead they made an example of his self-discipline and wisdom.

In a couple of hours Rayford would be the first to see hints of the sun, a teasing palette of pastels that would signal the reluctant dawn over the continent. Until then, the blackness through the window seemed miles thick. His groggy or sleeping passengers had window shades down, pillows and blankets in place. For now the plane was a dark, humming sleep chamber for all but a few wanderers, the attendants, and one or two responders to nature's call.

The question of the darkest hour before dawn, then, was whether Rayford Steele should risk a new, exciting relationship with Hattie Durham. He suppressed a smile. Was he kidding himself? Would someone with his reputation ever do anything but dream about a beautiful woman fifteen years his junior? He wasn't so sure anymore. If only Irene hadn't gone off on this new kick.

Would it fade, her preoccupation with the end of the world, with the love of Jesus, with the salvation of souls? Lately she had been reading everything she could get her hands on about the Rapture of the church. 'Can you imagine, Rafe,' she exulted, 'Jesus coming back to get us before we die?'

'Yeah, boy,' he said, peeking over the top of his newspaper, 'that would kill me.'

She was not amused. 'If I didn't know what would happen to me,' she said, 'I wouldn't be glib about it.'

'I *do* know what would happen to me,' he insisted. 'I'd be dead, gone, *finis*. But you, of course, would fly right up to heaven.'

He hadn't meant to offend her. He was just having fun. When she turned away he rose and pursued her. He spun her around and tried to kiss her, but she was cold. 'Come on, Irene,' he said. 'Tell me thousands wouldn't just keel over if they saw Jesus coming back for all the good people.'

She had pulled away in tears. 'I've told you and told you. Saved people aren't good people, they're –'

'Just forgiven, yeah, I know,' he said, feeling rejected and vulnerable in his own living room. He returned to his chair and his paper. 'If it makes you feel any better, I'm happy for you that you can be so cocksure.'

'I only believe what the Bible says,' Irene said.

Rayford shrugged. He wanted to say, 'Good for you,' but he didn't want to make a bad situation worse. In a way he had envied her confidence, but in truth he wrote it off to her being a more emotional, more feelings-oriented person. He didn't want to articulate it, but the fact was, he was brighter – yes, more intelligent. He believed in rules, systems, laws, patterns, things you could see and feel and hear and touch.

If God was part of all that, OK. A higher power, a loving being, a force behind the laws of nature, fine. Let's sing about it, pray about it, feel good about our ability to be kind to others, and go about our business. Rayford's greatest fear was that this religious fixation would not fade like Irene's Amway days, her Tupperware phase, and her aerobics spell. He could just see her ringing doorbells and asking if she could read people a verse or two. Surely she knew better than to dream of his tagging along.

Irene had become a full-fledged religious fanatic, and somehow that freed Rayford to daydream without guilt about Hattie Durham. Maybe he would say something, suggest something, hint at something as he and Hattie strode through Heathrow toward the cab line. Maybe earlier. Dare he assert himself even now, hours before touchdown?

Next to a window in first class, a writer sat hunched over his laptop. He shut down the machine, vowing to get back to his journal later. At thirty, Cameron Williams was the youngest ever senior writer for the prestigious *Global Weekly*. The envy of the rest of the veteran staff, he either scooped them on or was assigned to the best stories in the world. Both admirers and detractors at the magazine called him Buck, because they said he was always bucking tradition and authority. Buck believed he lived a charmed life, having been eyewitness to some of the most pivotal events in history.

A year and two months earlier, his January 1 cover story had taken him to Israel to interview Chaim Rosenzweig and had resulted in the most bizarre event he had ever experienced.

The elderly Rosenzweig had been the only unanimous choice for Newsmaker of the Year in the history of *Global Weekly*. Its staff had customarily steered clear of anyone who would be an obvious pick as *Time's Man of the Year*. *But Rosenzweig was an automatic. Cameron Williams had gone into the staff meeting prepared to argue for Rosenzweig and against whatever media star the others would typically champion.*

He was pleasantly surprised when executive editor Steve Plank opened with, 'Anybody want to nominate someone stupid, such as anyone other than the Nobel prizewinner in chemistry?'

The senior staff members looked at each other, shook their heads, and pretended to begin leaving. 'Put the chairs on the wagon, the meetin' is over,' Buck said. 'Steve, I'm not angling for it, but you know I know the guy and he trusts me.'

'Not so fast, Cowboy,' a rival said, then appealed to Plank. 'You letting Buck assign himself now?'

'I might,' Steve said. 'And what if I do?'

'I just think this is a technical piece, a science story,' Buck's detractor muttered. 'I'd put the science writer on it.'

'And you'd put the reader to sleep,' Plank said. 'C'mon, you know the writer for showcase pieces comes from this group. And this is not a science piece any more than the first one Buck did on him. This has to be told so the reader gets to know the man and understands the significance of his achievement.'

'Like that isn't obvious. It only changed the course of history.'

'I'll make the assignment today,' the executive editor said. 'Thanks for your willingness, Buck. I assume everyone else is willing as well.' Expressions of eagerness filled the room, but Buck also heard grumbled predictions that the fair-haired boy would get the nod. Which he did.

Such confidence from his boss and competition from his peers made him all the more determined to outdo himself with every assignment. In Israel, Buck stayed in a military compound and met with Rosenzweig in the same kibbutz on the outskirts of Haifa where he had interviewed him a year earlier.

Rosenzweig was fascinating, of course, but it was his discovery, or invention – no one knew quite how to categorize it – that was truly the 'newsmaker of the year.' The humble man called himself a botanist, but he was in truth a chemical engineer who had concocted a synthetic fertilizer that caused the desert sands of Israel to bloom like a greenhouse.

'Irrigation has not been a problem for decades,' the old man said. 'But all that did was make the sand wet. My formula, added to the water, fertilize the sand.'

Buck was not a scientist, but he knew enough to shake his head at that simple statement. Rosenzweig's formula was fast making Israel the richest nation on earth, far more profitable than its oil-laden neighbors. Every inch of ground blossomed with flowers and grains, including produce never before conceivable in Israel. The Holy Land became an export capital, the envy of the world, with virtually zero unemployment. Everyone prospered.

The prosperity brought about by the miracle formula changed the course of history for Israel. Flush with cash and resources, Israel made peace with her neighbors. Free trade and liberal passage allowed all who loved the nation to have access to it. What they did not have access to, however, was the formula.

Buck had not even asked the old man to reveal the formula or the complicated security process that protected it from any potential enemy. The very fact that Buck was housed by the military evidenced the importance of security. Maintaining that secret ensured the power and independence of the state of Israel. Never had Israel enjoyed such tranquility. The walled city of Jerusalem was only a symbol now, welcoming everyone who embraced peace. The old guard believed God had rewarded them and compensated them for centuries of persecution.

Chaim Rosenzweig was honored throughout the world and revered in his own country. Global leaders sought him out, and he was protected by security systems as complex as those that protected heads of state. As heady as Israel became with newfound glory, the nation's leaders were not stupid. A kidnapped and tortured Rosenzweig could be forced to reveal a secret that would similarly revolutionize any nation in the world.

Imagine what the formula might do if modified to work on the vast tundra of Russia! Could regions bloom, though snow covered most of the year? Was this the key to resurrecting that massive nation following the shattering of the Union of Soviet Socialist Republics?

Russia had become a great brooding giant with a devastated economy and regressed technology. All the nation had was military might, every spare mark going into weaponry. And the switch from rubles to marks had not been a smooth transition for the struggling nation. Streamlining world finance to three major currencies had taken years, but once the change was made, most were happy with it. All of Europe and Russia dealt exclusively in marks. Asia, Africa, and the Middle East traded in yen. North and South America and Australia dealt in dollars. A move was afoot to go to one global currency, but those nations that had reluctantly switched once were loath to do it again.

Frustrated at their inability to profit from Israel's fortune and determined to dominate and occupy the Holy Land, the Russians had launched an attack against Israel in the middle of the night. The assault became known as the Russian Pearl Harbor, and because of his interview with Rosenzweig, Buck Williams was in Haifa when it happened. The Russians sent intercontinental ballistic missiles and nuclear-equipped MiG fighter-bombers into the region. The number of aircraft and warheads made it clear their mission was annihilation.

To say the Israelis were caught off guard, Cameron Williams had written, was like saying the Great Wall of China was long. When Israeli radar picked up the Russian planes, they were nearly overhead. Israel's frantic plea for support from her immediate neighbors and the United States was simultaneous with her demand to know the intentions of the invaders of her airspace. By the time Israel and her allies could have mounted anything close to a defense, it was obvious the Russians would have her out-numbered a hundred to one.

They had only moments before the destruction would begin. There would be no more negotiating, no more pleas for a sharing of the wealth with the hordes of the north. If the Russians meant only to intimidate and bully, they would not have filled the sky with missiles. Planes could turn back, but the missiles were armed and targeted.

So this was no grandstand pay designed to bring Israel to her knees. There was no message for the victims. Receiving no explanation for war machines crossing her borders and descending upon her, Israel was forced to defend herself, knowing full well that the first volley would bring about her virtual disappearance from the face of the earth.

With warning sirens screaming and radio and television sending the doomed for what flimsy cover they might find, Israel defended herself for what would surely be the last time in history. The first battery of Israeli surface-to-air missiles hit their marks, and the sky was lit with orange-and-yellow balls of fire that would certainly do little to slow a Russian offensive for which there could be no defense.

Those who knew the odds and what the radar screens foretold interpreted the deafening explosions in the sky as the Russian onslaught. Every military leader who knew what was coming expected to be put out of his misery in seconds when the fusillade reached the ground and covered the nation.

From what he heard and saw in the military compound, Buck Williams knew the end was near. There was no escape. But as the night shone like day and the horrific, deafening explosions continued, nothing on the ground suffered. The building shook and rattled and rumbled. And yet it was not hit.

Outside, warplanes slammed to the ground, digging craters and sending burning debris flying. Yet lines of communication stayed open. No other command posts had been hit. No reports of casualties. Nothing destroyed yet.

Was this some sort of a cruel joke? Sure, the first Israeli missiles had taken out Russian fighters and caused missiles to explode too high to cause more than fire damage on the ground. But what had happened to the rest of the Russian air corps? Radar showed they had clearly sent nearly every plane they had, leaving hardly anything in reserve for defense. Thousands of planes swooped down on the tiny country's most populated cities.

The roar and the cacophony continued, the explosions so horrifying that veteran military leaders buried their faces and screamed in terror. Buck had always wanted to be near the front lines, but his survival instinct was on full throttle. He knew beyond doubt that he would die, and he found himself thinking the strangest thoughts. Why had he never married? Would there be remnants of his body for his father and brother to identify? Was there a God? Would death be the end?

He crouched beneath a console, surprised by the urge to sob. This was not at all what he had expected war to sound like, to look like. He had imagined himself peeking at the action from a safe spot, recording in his mind the drama.

Several minutes into the holocaust, Buck realized he would be no more dead outside than in. He felt no bravado, only uniqueness. He would be the only person in this post who would see and know what killed him. He made his way to a door on rubbery legs. No one seemed to notice or care to warn him. It was as if they had all been sentenced to death.

He forced open the door against a furnace blast and had to shield his eyes from the whiteness of the blaze. The sky was afire. He still heard planes over the din and roar of the fire itself, and the occasional exploding missile sent new showers of flame into the air. He stood in stark terror and amazement as the great machines of war plummeted to the earth all over the city, crashing and burning. But they fell between buildings and in deserted streets and fields. Anything atomic and explosive erupted high in the atmosphere, and Buck stood there in the heat, his face blistering and his body pouring sweat. What in the world was happening?

Then came chunks of ice and hailstones big as golf balls, forcing Buck to cover his head with his jacket. The earth shook and resounded, throwing him to the ground. Facedown in the freezing shards, he felt rain wash over him. Suddenly the only sound was the fire in the sky, and it began to fade as it drifted lower. After ten minutes of thunderous roaring, the fire dissipated, and scattered balls of flame flickered on the ground. The firelight disappeared as quickly as it had come. Stillness settled over the land.

As clouds of smoke wafted away on a gentle breeze, the night sky reappeared in its blue-blackness and stars shone peacefully as if nothing had gone awry.

Buck turned back to the building, his muddy leather jacket in his fist. The doorknob was still hot, and inside, military leaders wept and shuddered. The radio was alive with reports from Israeli pilots. They had not been able to get airborne in time to do anything but watch as the entire Russian air offensive seemed to destroy itself.

Miraculously, not one casualty was reported in all of Israel. Otherwise Buck might have believed some mysterious malfunction had caused missile and plane to destroy each other. But witnesses reported that it had been a firestorm, along with rain and hail and an earthquake, that consumed the entire offensive effort.

Had it been a divinely appointed meteor shower? Perhaps. But what accounted for hundreds and thousands of chunks of burning, twisted, molten steel smashing to the ground in Haifa, Jerusalem, Tel Aviv, Jericho, even Bethlehem – leveling ancient walls but not so much as scratching one living creature? Daylight revealed the carnage and exposed Russia's secret alliance with Middle Eastern nations, primarily Ethiopia and Libya.

Among the ruins, the Israelis found combustible material that would serve as fuel and preserve their natural resources for more than six years. Special task forces competed with buzzards and vultures for the flesh of the enemy dead, trying to bury them before their bones were picked clean and disease threatened the nation.

Buck remembered it vividly, as if it were yesterday. Had he not been there and seen it himself, he would not have believed it. And it took more than he had in him to get any reader of *Global Weekly* to buy it either.

Editors and readers had their own explanations for the phenomenon, but Buck admitted, if only to himself, that he became a believer in God that day. Jewish scholars pointed out passages from the Bible that talked about God destroying Israel's enemies with a firestorm, earthquake, hail, and rain. Buck was stunned when he read Ezekiel 38 and 39 about a great enemy from the north invading Israel with the help of Persia, Libya, and Ethiopia. More stark was that the Scriptures foretold of weapons of war used as fire fuel and enemy soldiers eaten by birds or buried in a common grave.

Christian friends wanted Buck to take the next step and believe in Christ, now that he was so clearly spiritually attuned. He wasn't prepared to go that far, but he was certainly a different person and a different journalist from then on. To him, nothing was beyond belief.

Not sure whether he'd follow through with anything overt, Captain Rayford Steele felt an irresistible urge to see Hattie Durham right then. He unstrapped himself and squeezed his first officer's shoulder on the way out of the cockpit. 'We're still on auto, Christopher,' he said as the younger man roused and straightened his headphones. 'I'm gonna make the sunup stroll.'

Christopher squinted and licked his lips. 'Doesn't look like sunup to me, Cap.'

'Probably another hour or two. I'll see if anybody's stirring anyway.'

'Roger. If they are, tell 'em Chris says, "Hey." '

Rayford snorted and nodded. As he opened the cockpit door, Hattie Durham nearly bowled him over.

'No need to knock,' he said. 'I'm coming.'

The senior flight attendant pulled him into the galleyway, but there was no passion in her touch. Her fingers felt like talons on his forearm, and her body shuddered in the darkness.

'Hattie –'

She pressed him back against the cooking compartments, her face close to his. Had she not been clearly terrified, he might have enjoyed this and returned her embrace. Her knees buckled as she tried to speak, and her voice came in a whiny squeal.

'People are missing,' she managed in a whisper, burying her head in his chest.

He took her shoulders and tried to push her back, but she fought to stay close. 'What do you m –?'

She was sobbing now, her body out of control. 'A whole bunch of people just gone!'

'Hattie, this is a big plane. They've wandered to the lavs or –'

She pulled his head down so she could speak directly into his ear. Despite her weeping, she was plainly fighting to make herself understood. 'I've been everywhere. I'm telling you, dozens of people are missing.'

'Hattie, it's still dark. We'll find –'

'I'm not crazy! See for yourself! All over the plane, people have disappeared.'

'It's a joke. They're hiding, trying to –'

'Ray! Their shoes, their socks, their clothes, everything was left behind. These people are gone!'

Hattie slipped from his grasp and knelt whimpering in the corner. Rayford wanted to comfort her, to enlist her help, or to get Chris to go with him through the plane. More than anything he wanted to believe the woman was crazy. She knew better than to put him on. It was obvious she really believed people had disappeared.

He had been daydreaming in the cockpit. Was he asleep now? He bit his lip hard and winced at the pain. So he was wide awake. He stepped into first class, where an elderly woman sat stunned in the predawn haze, her husband's sweater and trousers in her hands. 'What in the world?' she said. 'Harold?'

Rayford scanned the rest of first class. Most passengers were still asleep, including a young man by the window, his laptop computer on the tray table. But indeed several seats were empty. As Rayford's eyes grew accustomed to the low light, he strode quickly to the stairway. He started down, but the woman called to him.

'Sir, my husband –'

Rayford put a finger to his lips and whispered, 'I know. We'll find him. I'll be right back.'

What nonsense! he thought as he descended, aware of Hattie right behind him. *'We'll find him'?*

Hattie grabbed his shoulder and he slowed. 'Should I turn on the cabin lights?'

'No,' he whispered. 'The less people know right now, the better.'

Rayford wanted to be strong, to have answers, to be an example to his crew, to Hattie. But when he reached the lower level he knew the rest of the flight would be chaotic.

He was as scared as anyone on board. As he scanned the seats, he nearly panicked. He backed into a secluded spot behind the bulkhead and slapped himself hard on the cheek.

This was no joke, no trick, no dream. Something was terribly wrong, and there was no place to run. There would be enough confusion and terror without his losing control. Nothing had prepared him for this, and he would be the one everybody would look to. But for what? What was he supposed to do?

First one, then another cried out when they realized their seatmates were missing but that their clothes were still there. They cried, they screamed, they leaped from their seats. Hattie grabbed Rayford from behind and wrapped her hands so tight around his chest that he could hardly breathe. 'Rayford, what is this?'

He pulled her hands apart and turned to face her. 'Hattie, listen. I don't know any more than you do. But we've got to calm these people and get on the ground. I'll make some kind of an announcement, and you and your people keep everybody in their seats. OK?'

She nodded but she didn't look OK at all. As he edged past her to hurry back to the cockpit, he heard her scream. *So much for calming the passengers*, he thought as he whirled to see her on her knees in the aisle. She lifted a blazer, shirt and tie still intact. Trousers lay at her feet. Hattie frantically turned the blazer to the low light and read the name tag. 'Tony!' she wailed. 'Tony's gone!'

Rayford snatched the clothes from her and tossed them behind the bulkhead. He lifted Hattie by her elbows and pulled her out of sight. 'Hattie, we're hours from touch-down. We can't have a planeload of hysterical people. I'm going to make an announcement, but you have to do your job. Can you?'

She nodded, her eyes vacant. He forced her to look at him. 'Will you?' he said.

She nodded again. 'Rayford, are we going to die?'

'No,' he said. 'That I'm sure of.'

But he wasn't sure of anything. How could he know? He'd rather have faced an engine fire or even an uncontrolled dive. A crash into the ocean had to be better than this. How would he keep people calm in such a nightmare?

By now keeping the cabin lights off was doing more harm than good, and he was glad to be able to give Hattie a specific assignment. 'I don't know what I'm going to say,' he said, 'but get the lights on so we can make an accurate record of who's here and who's gone, and then get more of those foreign visitor declaration forms.'

'For what?'

'Just do it. Have them ready.'

Rayford didn't know if he had done the right thing by leaving Hattie in charge of the passengers and crew. As he raced up the stairs, he caught sight of another attendant backing out of a galleyway, screaming. By now poor Christopher in the cockpit was the only one on the plane unaware of what was happening. Worse, Rayford had told Hattie he didn't know what was happening any more than she did.

The terrifying truth was that he knew all too well. Irene had been right. He, and most of his passengers, had been left behind.

People of the Blessing

James Jones

In a world of stress and pressure, of shorter deadlines and instant communications, how can we enter into the blessing of God? James Jones, Bishop of Liverpool, offers reflections and meditations on selected Psalms to help us experience God's blessing and reveal His love to others.

ISBN: 1-84101-053-7

Price: £5.99

Copyright © 1991, 1998 James Jones

First published in 1991 by The Bible Reading Fellowship
Peter's Way, Sandy Lane West, Oxford OX4 5HG
Revised edition 1998

In Search of Blessing

Green Trees and Streams of Water
Psalm 1:1–6

Blessed is the man who has not walked in the counsel of the
ungodly:
nor followed the way of sinners
nor taken his seat amongst the scornful.
But his delight is in the law of the Lord:
and on that law he will ponder day and night.
He is like a tree planted beside streams of water:
that yields its fruit in due season.
Its leaves also shall not wither:
and look whatever he does it shall prosper.

As for the ungodly, it is not so with them:
they are like the chaff which the wind scatters.
Therefore the ungodly shall not stand up at the judgment:
nor sinners in the congregation of the righteous.
For the Lord cares for the way of the righteous:
but the way of the ungodly shall perish.

The Promise of Blessing

> *Blessed is the man who has not walked in the counsel of the*
> *ungodly:*
> *nor followed the way of sinners*
> *nor taken his seat amongst the scornful.*
> *But his delight is in the law of the Lord:*
> *and on that law he will ponder day and night.*

A Reflection

When in a city and with time to spare between appointments I often escape into a church. As I have passed through the great doors on a humid summer's day I have left behind the noise and heat, the fumes and the jostling crowds and entered the cool serenity of another world. Just feet away the urban fever still rages but here in this sanctuary there is space for renewal.

This first psalm provides for us the great west door into the book of psalms and into the blessing promised to those who will sit and ponder on the law of the Lord. It presents us with two worlds: the world of bedlam and the world of sanity. There are two ways: the way of destruction and the way of righteousness.

Do we fail to see that two such worlds exist? Do we fail to see that there are attitudes and aspirations at large that conflict with those of God? If so, this means that we have reached one of two situations. Either, Christian values have so permeated our culture that society has been effectively Christianized and the divide bridged. Or, Christians are so conformed to, and moulded by, their contemporaries that they have lost their distinctive grit.

This psalm comes to us as a personal stirring of the conscience to resist deliberately the influences of those who have voted God out of office. Such influences are strong, persuasive and insidious.

John Newton, even after his dramatic conversion to the Lord Jesus Christ, continued to command a slave-ship. He studied the Bible while ferrying slaves across the Atlantic, and prayed in his cabin while, feet beneath him, men and women died in the suffocating and disease-ridden bowels of his ship. It took the Holy Spirit a few more years to shake his servant out of the moral numbness induced by 'the counsel of the ungodly'.

Of course, we find such behaviour hard to believe. How could a committed Christian do such a thing? The point is that we need to ask the spirit of truth to diagnose our own blind spots. What will future generations view with incredulity when they examine the relationship of today's Church with the world?

The positive step that is held before us to counteract the negative influences is to delight in God's word and to meditate on his truths. Delight suggests something unhurried. In our hectic schedules we do not often leave time for the leisurely and time-consuming art of delighting. People who delight in a view do not quickly glance at it: they linger, reflect, absorb, savour, appreciate, and enjoy what they see. Their delighting both expresses and nourishes their character.

This psalm gives us a picture of such a person. He or she is like 'a tree planted beside streams of water; that yields its fruit in due season'. Meditate on this. Dwell on this picture. Imagine the hidden roots of the tree searching out the life-giving water. Look into the crystal-clear water of the stream. Feel its cold vigour. Taste its earthy and vital purity. Let yourself crave for the refreshment of such cooling streams; let your thirst for renewal be quenched as you take time to meditate on the promise of this psalm.

A Word from Jesus

Remember the words of Jesus:

> *'Let anyone who is thirsty come to me, and let the one who believes in me drink. As the scripture has said, "Out of the believer's heart shall flow rivers of living water." ' Now he said this about the Spirit . . . (John 7:37–39)*

A Meditation

Lord, I come.
Into the sanctuary of your presence I come.
Leaving behind for a while all the distractions of my daily life.
Lord, I come.

Lord, I come.
Sullied by compromise, flawed with self-centredness, soiled by sin.
Conscious that unconsciously I have absorbed
attitudes and values and aspirations
that are at odds with your unadulterated goodness,
your sheer beauty,
your healing purposes,
your compassionate justice.

Lord, I come.
Rid me of the sour taste of sin.

Lord, I come.
Wet my lips with the sweet taste of your word.
Cause me to savour every word,
glean every nuance,
cherish every sight of you.

Let the roots of my being go in search of you.
Let them be nourished by the cool waters of your Spirit.
Let your life renew my life.
Let your life satisfy.
Let your life be my blessing
And yield its fruit in due season.

Turmoil & Uncertainty
Psalm 2: 1–11

Why are the nations in tumult:
and why do the peoples cherish a vain dream?
The kings of the earth rise up
and the rulers conspire together;
against the Lord and against his anointed saying,
'Let us break their bonds asunder:
let us throw off their chains from us.'

He that dwells in heaven shall laugh them to scorn:
the Lord will hold them in derision.
Then he will speak to them in his wrath
and terrify them in his fury:
'I the Lord have set up my king on Zion my holy hill.'

I will announce the Lord's decree
That which he has spoken:
'You are my son, this day I have begotten you.
Ask of me
and I will give you the nations for your inheritance:
the uttermost parts of the earth for your possession.
You shall break them with a rod of iron:
and shatter them in pieces like a potter's vessel.'

> *Now therefore be wise O kings:*
> *be advised you that are judges of the earth.*
> *Serve the Lord with awe*
> *and govern yourselves in fear and trembling:*
> *lest he be angry and you perish in your course.*

The Promise of Blessing

> *For his wrath is quickly kindled:*
> *blessed are those that turn to him for refuge.*

A Reflection

The events of the late 1980s were as surprising as a sudden storm. Nobody ever imagined we would see the dismantling of the Berlin Wall and the disintegration of communist governments in Eastern Europe. It was unpredictable, and as relentless as an incoming tide. Even those hardline governments which seemed like castles set in concrete yielded and collapsed like sandcastles under the rising tide of populism. Yet on these beaches is now to be found the flotsam of uncertainty. There are the simmering tensions in Russia and the new republics, economic hardship in countries such as Albania, and the ongoing anguish of much of the former Yugoslavia. The nations of the world are still 'in tumult'.

It was in a similar situation of political and social upheaval that this psalm was written. In between the death of one king and the anointing of another there were often popular uprisings. Every change in government is marked by a degree of turmoil and uncertainty. This scenario provides the canvas on which the psalmist paints a picture of contrast between the political ambitions of people and the purposes of God.

The psalm was actually sung at the coronation of a new king. The first three verses speak about the kings of the earth and their political aspirations and strategies; the second set of verses is about the heavenly king who rules over the world; the third section imagines an ideal king who will rule a rebellious world with a rod of iron.

It is not difficult to see how the Jews, constantly disappointed by rulers who failed them and continually frustrated by the oppressive rulers of foreign powers, began to look forward to an 'anointed one' (this is the meaning of the word 'messiah', Hebrew in origin, and 'Christ', Greek in origin). The Lord's anointed would fulfil their aspirations for a kingdom of justice and peace.

The followers of Jesus began to see that Jesus himself was the Lord's anointed – the messiah or Christ – the one who would usher in God's Kingdom. That is why this psalm features so often in the New Testament about Jesus (see Matthew 3:17; 17:5; Acts 13:33; Hebrews 1:5; 5:5). When Jesus stood in front of Pilate at his trial, he recognized two things that are explicit in this psalm and important to note. Firstly, he said, 'My kingdom is not from this world' (John 18:36). This does not mean that Jesus' kingdom has nothing to do with this world. The words mean: 'My kingship does not derive from men and women.' It is God who designates and anoints Jesus as King (see Psalm 2:5–7). And although the kingship of Jesus does not derive from human election his kingdom is, without doubt, expected to extend to and touch every corner of the earth. Secondly, Jesus informs Pilate: 'You would have no power over me unless it had been given you from above' (John 19:11). Jesus recognized the ultimate sovereignty of God over all human affairs (see Psalm 2:4). God is in control even though at times the course of events takes an unpredictable or even bizarre turn.

Because power corrupts and absolute power corrupts absolutely, it is life-saving that those in power (in the world, society, companies, unions, households, local communities) remember the warning of Jesus to Pilate that they are accountable in the end to God. 'Serve the Lord with awe and govern yourselves in fear and trembling' (Psalm 2:10). As we rejoice at the ending of harsh dictatorships we must pray that they do not give rise to a different form of godless oppression: 'For his wrath is quickly kindled: blessed are those that turn to him for refuge' (Psalm 2:11).

A Word from Jesus

At his baptism there was,

> *A voice from heaven saying: 'This is my Son, the Beloved, with whom I am well pleased'* (Matthew 3:17).

At his transfiguration,

> *A voice from the cloud said: 'This is my Son, the Beloved; with him I am well pleased'* (Matthew 17:5).

There was no such comforting voice from heaven when Jesus died alone upon the cross. Yet because of his passion and death we may now hear the Lord of heaven and earth say to each of *us*: 'This is my beloved child, with whom I am well pleased.'

A Prayer

Lay before you the world news of a daily newspaper. Read each of the stories' headlines, then praise God.

Blessed be the name of God from age to age,
for wisdom and power are his.
He changes times and seasons,
deposes kings and sets up kings;
he gives wisdom to the wise
and knowledge to those who have understanding.
He reveals deep and hidden things;
he knows what is in the darkness,
and light dwells with him. (Daniel 2:20–22)

Portrait of Perfection
Psalm 24:1–10

The earth is the Lord's and the fullness thereof,
the world and those who dwell therein;
for he has founded it upon the seas,
and established it upon the rivers.

Who shall ascend the hill of the Lord?
And who shall stand in his holy place?
He who has clean hands and a pure heart,
who does not lift up his soul to what is false,
and does not swear deceitfully.
He will receive blessing from the Lord,
and vindication from the God of his salvation.
Such is the generation of those who seek him,
who seek the face of the God of Jacob.

Lift up your heads, O gates!
and be lifted up, O ancient doors!
that the King of glory may come in.
Who is the King of glory?
The Lord, strong and mighty,
the Lord, mighty in battle!
Lift up your heads, O gates!
and be lifted up, O ancient doors!

> *that the King of glory may come in.*
> *Who is this King of glory?*
> *The Lord of hosts,*
> *he is the King of glory!*

The Promise of Blessing

> *He will receive blessing from the Lord,*
> *and vindication from the God of his salvation.*

A Reflection

This is a psalm about entering into the worship of God. The verse which precedes the promise of blessing is daunting for any with an awareness of the dark side of their nature:

> *He who has clean hands and a pure heart,*
> *who does not lift up his soul to what is false,*
> *and does not swear deceitfully.*

Here is a portrait of perfection that tells the aspiring worshipper who is flawed by sin that there is no space for the likes of him in the 'holy place'! Who on earth has clean hands, a pure heart, never lies nor breaks a promise? It has been said that if we could devise a camera to photograph our thoughts then none of us would have a friend in the world! Many of us are grateful that our heart is not worn on our sleeve and that, for the most part, it remains well hidden. Yet it is God who knows our hearts and nothing can be hidden from him.

Purity for the Jewish worshippers was secured by the high priest entering the Holy Place in the temple and offering a sacrifice on behalf of the people. The sacrifice was an effective prayer that both sought and assured them of the forgiveness of God. Now through the sacrificial death of Jesus, God forgives us uniquely and eternally. 'And every priest stands day after day at his service, offering again and again the same sacrifices that can never take away sins.' But when Christ had offered for all time a single sacrifice for sins, 'he sat down at the right hand of God' . . . and the Holy Spirit also testifies to us . . . 'I will remember their sins and their lawless deeds no more' . . . Therefore, my friends, since we have confidence to enter the sanctuary by the blood of Jesus . . . let us approach with a true heart in full assurance of faith, with our hearts sprinkled clean from an evil conscience and our bodies washed with pure water' (Hebrews 10:11, 12, 15, 17, 19, 22). Through Jesus we can find clean hands and a pure heart and enter fully into the worship of God.

This psalm also speaks about the gates of the temple being opened to the King of Glory and imagines God taking his place upon his throne, the ark, at the heart of the temple.

The Christian believer is encouraged to see himself and the Christian community as the new temple in which the Lord by his Spirit resides (see 1 Corinthians 6:19, 20 and 2 Corinthians 6:16–18). This truth is often captured in the image of us asking the risen Christ to enter our hearts. But this sort of language and imagery can sometimes be misleading, especially for children with whom it is most often used.

A few years ago, when my three teenage daughters were much younger, I remember one day when they were jumping all over me as I was lying on the floor. When I protested at yet another blow to my solar plexus, 'Please, don't jump on Daddy's tummy,' one of my daughters piped up in my defence, 'No, or you'll squash Jesus!' But, although such talk about asking Jesus into our hearts can lead to misunderstanding, it does reflect a biblical spirituality that ought not to be neglected.

The apostle Paul, writing to the factious Christians at Corinth, urges: 'Examine yourselves to see whether you are living in the faith. Test yourselves. Do you not realize that Jesus Christ is in you? – unless, indeed, you fail to pass the test!' (2 Corinthians 13:5).

There are at least two ways of defining a Christian. One is to see Jesus as your example, the model of all that is good and pure to which you aspire. The other is to experience the Spirit of Jesus living within you. Both are biblical definitions. The latter is captured by John in a vision in the Book of Revelation when he hears the Spirit of Jesus say: 'I reprove and discipline those whom I love. Be earnest, therefore, and repent. Listen! I am standing at the door, knocking; if you hear my voice and open the door, I will come in to you and eat with you, and you with me' (Revelation 3:19, 20). These words were spoken to church people in a city called Laodicea. They challenged them to adopt a spirituality that experienced the indwelling of God's Spirit. Many of us who go to church often lack this dynamic experience. The simple solution is to take Jesus at his word and, like the Jewish worshippers who opened wide the gates of the temple, open the door of your heart and let the King of Glory come in. There and then you will 'receive the blessing from the Lord'. For, what is blessing other than communion with the King of Glory?

A Word from Jesus

Jesus said,

'*Those who love me will keep my word, and my Father will love them, and we will come to them and make our home with them*' *(John 14:23).*

A Meditation

Imagine a door to our inner being, your soul, your heart.
This is the place of your dreams,
your ambitions,
your feelings,
your will.
Imagine Jesus standing beyond the door, as the King of Glory.
Imagine his light shining all around you. Imagine the door of
your heart closed
to him, shutting out the light.
Imagine the darkness that shrouds your dreams,
your ambitions,
your feelings,
your will.
Weep for the gates that bar the King of Glory.
Say:
'Lift up your heads, O gates!
and be lifted up, O ancient doors!
that the King of Glory may come in.'
Open the gates. Open wide the door of your heart.
The king of glory shall come in.
The king of glory has come in.
Hallelujah!

The Blessing of Forgiveness
Psalm 32:1–5

Blessed is he
whose transgressions are forgiven,
whose sins are covered.
Blessed is the man
whose sin the Lord does not count against him
and in whose spirit is no deceit.

When I kept silent,
my bones wasted away
through my groaning all day long.
For day and night
your hand was heavy upon me;
my strength was sapped
as in the heat of summer.
Then I acknowledged my sin to you
and did not cover up my iniquity.
said, 'I will confess
transgressions to the Lord' –
and you forgave
the guilt of my sin.

The Promise of Blessing

> *Blessed is he*
> *whose transgressions are forgiven,*
> *whose sins are covered.*

A Reflection

When I was a vicar I used to lead groups for those exploring the Christian faith. In one such group we were talking about God's offer of forgiveness when someone objected, 'Why do you keep emphasizing forgiveness? I don't need forgiveness.' I was startled as this person interrupted my flow of Christian doctrine, and was reminded yet again of the chasm that exists between Christians and those who do not share their view of the world. I gathered myself and lobbed a measured question by return.

'Have you never hurt another human being?'

'Oh, yes, of course,' she replied, more subdued.

'Then surely you need the forgiveness of those you've hurt. And you need the forgiveness of the one who made you.'

Our experience of the need for forgiveness is known by another word, guilt. Unfortunately, this idea has fallen on hard times. Some dismiss guilt as a neurosis. Some criticize Christianity for placing an unhealthy emphasis on guilt in order to keep people in the church. But guilt is the normal experience of men and women who are morally responsible for themselves. Some may wallow in guilt; some may experience guilt out of all proportion to their wrongdoing. These conditions may well be described as neurotic and require therapy. But a morally healthy human being ought to experience guilt when he does something wrong. Let's take an extreme example. If a rapist when convicted acknowledges no sense of guilt at his appalling crime then he is even less of a human being than his actions reveal. It is our human experience of guilt that paradoxically reveals our dignity as morally responsible persons. Although our culture is very coy about guilt and some counsellors dismiss it as unhealthy, the Bible clearly sees it as essential to our humanity.

All of us experience the need for forgiveness. There is not one soul on the face of the earth who has not needlessly hurt another person. We all need forgiveness. We all know what guilt is. 'Transgressions' means kicking over the traces. 'Trespassers will be prosecuted.' There is a line and nobody is allowed to go beyond it. If anyone crosses the line, he is a trespasser, a transgressor. God has drawn the line for us in the Ten Commandments and the Sermon on the Mount. Anyone who violates these laws is a trespasser and transgressor and needs God's forgiveness.

The good news which is trailed here and the broadcast by Jesus is that God is *willing* to forgive us. I used to think that God was a reluctant forgiver but when I became a father I discovered otherwise. Whenever my children kick over the traces and deliberately do something wrong I create a situation so that they can say sorry, so that I can forgive them, and we can be one again. God does not begrudge us his forgiveness. On the contrary, the extravagant generosity of his love impelled him to give us Jesus, our saviour and forgiver.

The picture given to us in this psalm is that the unforgiven soul is a restless, peaceless and dis-eased creature. The symptoms of his spiritual malaise are even physical. But

God's forgiveness is there for the asking. Many of us seek peace for our souls in the strangest of places. It is only in journeying to 'the green hill' of Calvary, where we find our Lord crucified, that we find the forgiveness of our sins, the remission of our guilt and peace eternal for our souls. Will you come? There is blessing to be found.

A Word from Jesus

After a sinful woman had anointed and bathed his feet at the house of Simon the Pharisee,

> *Then he said to her, 'Your sins are forgiven . . . go in peace' (Luke 7:48, 50).*

A Prayer

> *Lord,*
> *I have kept silent too long.*
> *I have presumed upon your kindness.*
> *I have left undone those things I should have done*
> *and have done those things I should not have done.*
> *I have kicked over the traces*
> *through my own deliberate fault.*
> *I have spoken words of destruction.*
> *I have painted pictures with my mind*
> *that would shame my closest friend.*
> *I have done that which is evil in your sight.*
> *Peace and blessing have been strangers to me.*
> *Instead of seeking your face I have sought excuses.*
> *Instead of confessing my transgression*
> *I have sought to justify myself.*
> *Instead of coveting your forgiveness*

I have comforted myself with vanities:
'It's natural', 'I'm human', 'Everybody is like it'.
Lord, I confess my transgression.

Lord Jesus, have mercy on me.

My child,
I forgive you.
The guilt is gone.
Go in peace.
The blessing is yours.
Rejoice.